Emmanuel: God-With-Us

Emmanuel: God-With-Us

Reflections on the
Mystery of Christmas

by
Fr. John C. Cusick

Emmanuel: God-With-Us

Copyright © 2021 Fr. John C. Cusick

10 9 8 7 6 5 4 3 2 1

ISBN 978-1-7352702-4-1

Published by
CORBY BOOKS
A Division of Corby Publishing, LP

P.O. Box 93
Notre Dame, IN 46556

Manufactured in the United States of America

This Book is Dedicated to
Florence A. Cusick

She gave birth to her first-born son and
wrapped him in a swaddling clothes.
1945

Thank you, David Kovacs, for the time you have given to make these Christmas Reflections evolve into book form. Thanks, too, for organizing this material, for your many suggestions, and for your gift of editing my thoughts and ideas.

Thank you, Wina Shelley. You have been blessed with many gifts and talents. Thanks for creating the Illustrations that make this a much better little book.

- John Cusick

About These Pages...

EACH YEAR during the weeks before Christmas I scan through the stories surrounding the birth of Christ that are found in the early chapters of the Gospels of Matthew and Luke. I begin by looking for insights that would lead to a Christmas homily.

After a few years, that changed. I began to find insights not only for preaching but also for my own spiritual journey through life. And, amazingly, those same two Gospel stories reveal new and different insights year-after-year. Over twenty-five years ago I chose to write down my reflections. Many are found within these pages.

The religious imagery in these birth narratives of Emmanuel: God-With-Us is wonderful—a king in fear of a child; a virgin bearing a son; the bottom of the social ladder (shepherds) the first to get good news; a newborn wrapped in the symbol of love: swaddling clothes; a savior of the world (Caesar Augustus) and a savior of the world (the Christ child); peace through armies; peace through Shalom among people of good will—through the healing of human relationships;

angels singing; shepherds preaching; no need for room in an inn when you are home: Bethlehem—the house of bread, home of the bread of life; salvation resting in a manger—a feeding trough—here, take and eat; this is my body.

I also discovered that these images surrounding Christ's birth connected me to my memories of Christmas throughout my life. As I pull out my crib from under my bed and put it under my Christmas tree, I remember walking with my mom to Anthony's 5 & 10-cent store on 79th street to buy a manger. I can recall asking her for some spare change in the years to come so that I could buy a few more sheep. And still today, just like when I was a little kid, I hang the star and arrange the sheep next to those shepherds. I place Mary and Joseph on either side of Jesus in the manger. I make sure the camels are all in place and then decide which magi's gift will be the first one to be given to Jesus this year. I remember gifts I received from my mom and dad and gifts I gave to them. So much of my life comes alive in reflecting on the Christmas story.

Before you read these reflections, you may wish to reread the event of the birth of Christ in Matthew and Luke. Set the stage for yourself. Allow all these amazing descriptions and images to come alive for you. Read the texts slowly. You might even want to read to stories out loud. It is amazing what you might hear. Stop when necessary to reflect when something you have seen and read a thousand times before is revealed as a new and first-time insight. You may even want to write it down. I did and that is what has led to the pages that follow.

May you enjoy reading these reflections as much as I have enjoyed writing them each year.

Fr. John Cusick
CHRISTMAS, 2021

Contents

CHAPTER 7

PEACE ON EARTH

CHAPTER 8

GIFTS

CHAPTER 9

'TIS THE SEASON:
   TAKE CARE OF SOME PEOPLE

CHAPTER 10
TRADITIONS

CHAPTER 11
SING WITH ME

CHAPTER 1

Emmanuel – God-With-Us

Christmas –
The Mystery of Faith!

Emmanuel...

It seems that the word, that name, dropped into the human community about 2200 years ago. It was a reminder and reassurance that "God is with us." Those were turbulent times with imminent wars on the horizon. Isaiah the prophet reminded those who led the people that God will be with His people: Emmanuel.

...God-With-Us

About seven or eight centuries later that name, Emmanuel, reappeared in a dream between a humble man and a divine messenger. And this time when it arrived in that dream, the Gospel of Matthew gave Emmanuel an interpretation of its meaning: *"Behold, a virgin shall be with child, and shall bring forth a son, and they shall call his name Emmanuel, which being interpreted is, God with us."*

3

Now, every year we revisit this time-honored name and title. Now we apply it to an amazing revelation: that a virgin named Mary birthed a son who in fact was Emmanuel, God-With-Us.

It is the drama of Christmas. It is God's gift to us. It is a Christmas gift like no other.

Wrapped in swaddling clothes.

The Lord God even wrapped His gift to us. No, not in bright paper with bells and bows.

God has wrapped his Emmanuel in love, swaddling clothes—just like King Solomon, "*In swaddling clothes and with constant care I was nurtured*" (Wisdom 7:4). The Baby was wrapped in love like a King of Israel. Emmanuel came to as a gift from God wrapped tightly in love.

Lying in a manger.

His first resting place was not a bassinet or tiny crib. Wrapped in love, Emmanuel, God-With-Us, wrapped tightly in love was first placed in a manger, a feeding trough for animals! Yes. From the first day of his young life, he was depicted as being food for others. Here take and eat. This is my body. Now that's Emmanuel—God-With-Us!

Glory to God! And on earth peace to those on whom God's favor rests.

God loves us. His favor rests on us. It is this child wrapped in Love. Here. It is for you.

Oh, it is so sad to hear people say they know God's will. Then then dominate, injure, even kill people in the name of God. That is not Emmanuel. That is not His offering of love. That is not His food that gives life to people. It a not personal possession for you or me alone. It is not a secret. It is not buried treasure.

This Christmas gift that is wrapped so beautifully in swaddling clothes is Emmanuel, God-With-Us. It is a gift for all of us—for all of humankind. It is a gift that keep us giving—each and every day. It is a gift of love and presence that must be shared and lived by us. That is what it means to know the will of God.

There is no violence in Emmanuel. There is no hatred or bigotry in "God-With-Us." There is only communion, and love, and peace on whom His favor rests.

Again, this year can you sense that Emmanuel is with is wrapped in love as food for all? Just say amen.

Amen!

Merry Christmas!

I Am Your God.
You are My People.

CHRISTMAS MEANS SO MUCH. It is filled with...

Memories—of family and good times.

Nostalgia—of those early Christmases.

Hope—for even better times for us and everyone.

Longing—that maybe this year a better world can happen.

Christmas: It is filled with a tremendous sense of faith.

"The Word was made flesh and dwells with us." God and humankind as one. The Glory of God among us.

Christmas: A celebration of where God always has been... in, with and among God's people since the beginning of time.

The God of our ancestors—who announced a Presence and a dream to Abraham: *"I will surely bless you and make your descendants as numerous as the stars in the sky and as the sand on the seashore."*

The God of the Covenant—*"I am your God. You are my people."*

The God who dwelled with them—led them on, shared their history, forgave their sins, called them to Life.

Christmas—the Word was made flesh and dwelt with them. An encounter with God that reveals to us all that our history and our lives are not in vain, not meaningless existences with no hope or future.

"*The Word became flesh.*" The sign that God is with us, one with us. We never again need to look to any other place for God - not into the heavens, the sunset, sparkling brooks, or snow -capped mountains. We simply need to see God in ourselves and in all whom we encounter.

Christmas—God is with us, never to leave us.

Think of what that does to us. What an unbelievable sense of dignity that gives us. What grace and style we have inherited.

Oh, it is true we tend to hide God's Presence at times. Our insensitivity, our use and abuse of power, the ways we can manipulate others to get our way, our hardness of heart. But in spite of it all, Christmas says God is present, always and forever. If that is so, then we can never say that God does not understand.

The Christmas Spirit

YOU HEAR A LOT about it this time of year. It is something you are supposed to have. As a matter of fact, everyone is supposed to have it.

The Christmas Spirit!

That's what the season is all about. Yet, it isn't seasonal.

Some say that you will appreciate it with a little snow. Yet, it doesn't come from the clouds above.

Others contend it is brought on by the colorful ornaments, twinkling lights and festive decorations. The more of those things you display, the better you will be. Probably not. Its impact is not that flashy.

Kids. Expose yourself to the wonders of children this time of the year. You can catch it from them. They can make it contagious. Yet, there is some question if it can be passed from one to another.

Amazingly, we are never without it. Any season, any mood, any lifestyle.

It's the Christmas Spirit. We call it to mind now.

We celebrate it with colors, lights, songs and story. But it is not in those things.

The Christmas Spirit is within us—within all of humankind.

In recalling the birth of the God Child, we discover our Christmas Spirit.

In the very center of life itself, within each and every one of us, God dwells.

In that center, in the spirit-side of us, we too, are wrapped in love, like that Child wrapped in swaddling clothes.

Aren't we our best self, when we care for others? In a way don't we become like food and drink for them?

"*You will find him lying in a manger.*" In a feeding trough you will find him, to be food and life and care for others.

Yes, it is the Christmas Spirit.

We are never without it. It grows within us. It can be borne by us into the world of others.

It will not go away, no matter what time of the year. It loves you so that you may love others.

It's the Christmas Spirit!

It's that seasonal greeting to remind us of the never-ending activity of God. Believe it. Birth it.

"Merry Christmas!"
More than Just a Greeting

"MERRY CHRISTMAS!"

I used that greeting the other day. And, you know what? It sounded real good!

And it felt good, too.

It is a salutation that is spoken less frequently today than ever before. It has taken a cultural back seat to "Happy Holidays."

I am okay with that.

Christmas is not the feast of retail America or the office holiday party. It is not the greeting of just anyone.

"Merry Christmas" is *my* greeting to you and to all I meet.

It is the spiritual joy, when those who gather in Jesus name, wish God's human presence to the world and to all people.

"Merry Christmas" is my announcement that the dream of Isaiah, "...*The virgin shall conceive and bear a*

11

son and call him Emmanuel (God-with-us)," has become human in the Lord Jesus.

"Merry Christmas" is the proclamation that God is with us; life is good and our lives can be different.

"Merry Christmas" is my wish that the divine activity birthed in Bethlehem can bring communion to a world and families of nations filled with division.

"Merry Christmas" is my hope that someday, please God, the announcement of God's peace will take root in presidents and prime ministers, in terrorists and soldiers, in gangbangers and power brokers, in talk show hosts and televangelists, in abusers and abused and in everyone of good will.

"Merry Christmas!"

What a wonderful dream!

Merry Christmas to you!

The Word Was Made Flesh

WHAT A GREAT invention the human mind is.

It allows us to remember our past, and many other people's pasts, too. It allows us the privilege to wonder about the future. We can dream, daydream and brainstorm.

And through the screen of our mind, we can "see" what it all looks like, too.

The mind allows us to tell stories to teach others and to crack jokes to add humor to life. We can recall what people like in order to please them, and, if we want, retrieve incidents to embarrass them.

But sometimes it is not enough simply to remember, reminisce, dream or brainstorm. It is time to act.

No idea in the mind, no memory between our ears, has ever changed a single thing in life. It must become real and active. It must take flesh. It must be seen.

The Word was made flesh.

The stories of God and God's people, the stories of love, forgiveness and promise were repeated from the minds of people for years and years.

They based their lives on those stories, made them a part of their very lives, retold them so as to never forget them, and knew that God would never forget them.

Forget them? God didn't.

Forget us? God won't.

The Word was made flesh. No longer a memory in story, but the flesh of life. God's presence takes on a new and powerful meaning: One with us. Present to us. Dwelling with us.

From the memory of Bethlehem to our activity today, the Word is made flesh.

The Word was made flesh and dwells among us.

A God who dwells among the pain, stands by our loneliness, thrills in our joy, shares our life.

Our life. Not somebody else more beautiful, more successful, more popular.

You and me—us. *The Word was made flesh and dwells among us.*

Us: you and me.

That is Christmas!

I Wonder as I Wander
Out Under the Sky

I WONDER about a lot of things. I always have.

I have been blessed with a very fertile mind and imagination.

As an only child, I wondered about and even created lots of things between my ears. I remember taking an empty refrigerator packing box and making it into a rocket ship ready to blast off into outer space.

These days I stand in the dark in my back yard on a starry, starry night and simply looking up in awe and wonder into outer space, into the firmament of the heavens.

At another time in life I was standing in front of a bronze mural depicting school-age children of color whose clothes and skin were being torn by high-powered fire hoses aimed at them by police personnel. They were children...innocent, powerless and pure.

I wonder how anyone could do that.

I wonder if I can do more and say more to speak truth to bigotry.

Holding a newborn, I wonder about what lies ahead for this little person. I wonder what contribution to the world will be made by this innocent one. I wonder what kind of world this child will inherit from the likes of me.

I wonder why God so loves this world.

I wonder what is happening to truth telling.

I wonder why so many are so mean.

I wonder why the Son of God's dream is to give us life in abundance.

I wonder if I might be more than I seem.

I wonder why this Son is like us...in all things but sin.

I wonder what the baby in the manger saw on a starry, starry night.

I wonder if the Child wondered about similar things as I wondered, as he grew in age, wisdom and grace.

In a world that has little room for imagination and wonder, where crass pragmatism rules the day, where "show me" challenges faith, I find a particular joy and a much needed peace for my soul, when I am retold the story of the Wonder Counselor, Mighty God, Prince of Peace, born among us, wrapped in love, lying in a place that reveals he is food for the life and future of the world.

Yes. I wonder about the possibility of it all.

I always will.

CHAPTER 2

Advent

Get Ready!

GET READY.

It's about to happen again.

No. Not just Christmas.

But letting go. Inside and outside.

When you let go, mind you, let go just a little. It's a tough world. Much is expected of you. There's not much time to waste on fantasy and fascination.

Now, it's time again to sing, read, listen and pray about a child-God, angels speaking and people responding, a star in pursuit of a new-born, wise men on their knees at the feet of commoners.

It's incredible, isn't it? And it's about to happen again, whether you like it or not.

In a dog-eat-dog world, where getting things done is of prime importance, doesn't it seem a little odd to get all fired up about angels, a star and a child-God?

But there's much more to us than meets the eye. We are Believers. We believe there is much more to life than meets the eye.

We believe in a child-God, a human-God, a dying-God an eternal-God, and a rising-God.

We believe that the heavens and the earth are intimately connected.

So, what's the big deal, in a dog-eat-dog world, about singing angels?

We have no problem that the raw, absolute, tough power of a king, a boss or anyone should fear innocence, justice and peace.

We believe that no one is too big or famous to bow down in front of the poor, the lowly or the little people.

We are Believers this season of the year. We believe in what can be. We believe there is a wholeness to creation: the celestial, the terrestrial and God.

Get ready. It's about to happen again.

You're a Believer. Let go now...just a little. It's about to begin again.

Another Christmas.

I'm Not There Yet

No. Not yet.

Yes. Christmas is coming, but it is the "Merry" part that is eluding me.

The glitz and glitter, colored lights in homes, offices, streets, decorated trees, the ringing of Salvation Army bells are not moving my spirit right now.

Merry is still missing.

In my search for Merry, I am coming to realize I am looking in the wrong places. I read, listen to, and watch too much news. I am experiencing a sense of personal powerlessness and cultural sadness.

But I think I am beginning to turn the corner.

I will not let the world outside of me possess me. I will not let it bring me down.

I almost forgot what I can bring to daily life!

In search for the adjective this year I have neglected the noun: Christmas. It's not the trees and the lights. It's the swaddling clothes and the manger. And the news? It is not a 24/7 cycle of sadness and bitterness.

The news is The Good News.

"Do not be afraid, Mary, you have found favor with God. Behold, you will conceive in your womb and bear a son, and you shall name him Jesus. The child to be born will be called holy, the Son of God."

And there is more Good News!

"The angel of the Lord appeared to the shepherds and said, 'Do not be afraid! For behold I proclaim to you good news of great joy for all the people. For today in the city of David, a savior has been born for you who is Messiah and Lord. And this will be a sign to you: you will find a child wrapped in swaddling clothes lying in a manger.'"

That's not denying the daily news cycle that can take your breath away. But that news doesn't end with: *This is the Gospel of the Lord.*

The Good News shared by Luke is telling us: Don't forget the other story, the rest of the story.

In spite of the one and because of the other, I feel an adjective and noun coming together...again!

Yes. It will be Merry. It will be a Merry Christmas. So be it!

Christmas Happens

LIKE CLOCKWORK.

Christmas happens every year...same date, same time.

Personal, social or world events can't stop it, or even slow its arrival. December 25th is the date, no matter our attitude or what events might be having an effect on us or on our world.

Christmas can, however, have a profound effect on us. As a religious feast, it becomes a way—just for a little while—of looking at life and maybe even trying to live life a different way.

And with this religious feast of Christmas we use spiritual images to help us interpret the happenings within us and around us this year and every year.

The event of Christmas on December 25, 1914 allowed enemies to sing together and exchange greetings of Christmas peace before they began killing each other on December 26th.

"A light shone in the darkness and the darkness could not comprehend it."

"I bring you news of great joy—a savior has been born to you, one who will save the world from its sins."

"You will find a child wrapped in swaddling clothes."

We can look at life today out of the eyes of light in a time of darkness. We might sense an experience of human hopefulness, just when the seemingly endless cycle of violence and human hatred hold the upper hand.

And when we sense we are becoming surrounded by the grip of indifference and routine, we celebrate on December 25th human life wrapped in love, not vengeance or terror...which we are told is news of great joy for ALL the people.

Quick! Christmas is happening. Right here. Right now.

See: the light in the dark.

Listen: for the good news of great joy.

Live: in such a way that ALL the people can get and live the message of Emmanuel—God with us.

Don't be afraid to say it or to wish it.

Merry Christmas!

But How?

THERE ARE FOUR wishes of the season: Peace, Hope, Joy, Love. They are called the Spirit of the Season.

In many places of religious neutrality, public schools, businesses, corporate offices, public places, these wishes have taken the place of the traditional greeting, "Merry Christmas!"

There's a problem, however, with Peace, Hope, Joy and Love. We're not told how to achieve them.

Oh, yes we are: Merry Christmas!

The experience and story of Christmas are our path to Peace, Hope, Joy and Love.

A Path to Peace:

Caesar Augustus was given the title Savior of the World. Emperors bring peace with armies and violence.

"A Savior has been born to you, the Messiah and Lord," announced the angels.

A bearer of Shalom, one who will bring people together: no oppression, no domination, no fear.

A Sign of Hope:

"And you, Bethlehem, land of Judah, from you shall come a ruler who will shepherd my people Israel."

One who will bring us life will lead us. One like us, an ordinary person.

A Symbol of Joy:

"You have nothing to fear! I come to proclaim good news to you—tidings of great joy!"

The feeling and knowledge that we are so blessed, that life is good, the future filled with great possibilities.

An Embrace of Love:

"You will find a child wrapped in swaddling clothes."

To be wrapped in swaddling clothes is to be wrapped in love. The child is wrapped in God's love. So are we God's children today. And we will wrap the world in the love of God.

We really can. We really will.

A path, a sign, a symbol, an embrace: Peace, Hope, Joy, Love.

Merry Christmas!

Not in Ordinary Time

CHRISTMAS.

If we are happy, we are ecstatically so. If we hurt, it is deeper hurt "this time of the year."

Christmas.

We seem to take less for granted. We "feel" for the poor and outcast. We might even cry in the sight of headlines reporting violence. We find ourselves asking "why" to war. We are ever so grateful for those with whom we live each day.

The little gifts are just loaded with meaning.

The smiles, embraces, kisses, glances, tears, and laughter allow more feeling out than usual.

Christmas.

It's wonder, awe and gratitude...all in a prominent place.

Christmas.

The marvelous always happens. Wild possibilities become real. The Christmas story is about lowly people giving birth to the "greatest of God." A king living in fear of an innocent child. Shepherds being stunned by visions of peace and a new order. Wise men kneel-ing in awe before a helpless child.

Christmas.

That is how God happens in daily life:

Innocent...yet powerfully.

Unexpected...yet sought out.

Quietly...yet proclaimed joyously.

Christmas.

It is just not an ordinary time of the year.

But then, the activity of God never is.

A Savior is Born to You:
Christ the Lord

LIFE: it is habit forming.

Christmas is all about life. Pure and simple.

Life: Inside the gifts, hidden in the half-tones of the bells, understood between the verses of the carols, revealed in the magic of the season, powered in the glitter of the lights…

Implied in each "Merry Christmas."

Life: what we take for granted so often.

Life: what we feel so intensely at Christmas.

Family. Poor people. Friends. Those we dislike.

The good news. The disappointments. The tears of wonder. The moments of regret. The merriment. The isolation. The possibility.

A Savior is born to you.

The wonder of life. The fascination of new life. New hopes and new promises.

A Savior is born to you.

New life: a chance almost to start again.

A Savior is born to you, Christ the Lord.

Imagine. God and us in this together. Born to us. Life.

In the routine of April, in the intensity of December, a Savior shares this time, this life with us.

It is Christ the Lord!

We Need Christmas

IT'S THE ONE SEASON of the year that has its own everything.

It has its own music, art, colors and stories. It seems to have a most positive effect on all of us.

The little kid in each of us is just waiting to break out...again.

We want to sing, to stand in awe of decorations, to give gifts, to be surprised. To make sure others are cared for, to dream of what could be: Christmas.

Maybe: No more war; less violence, more love, no poverty, less pain.

We need Christmas.

Just maybe...when times are tough, when we sense the harshness of reality, when we come up against limits, when we're told to grin and bear it, we need Christmas.

We need the great imagination and stories of what could be.

More than that.

We need the experience, day by day, of what life can be.

We need Christmas.

We need to realize that God is breaking forth in life, when you sense that it could be different, when you are surprised, when you are generous, when you care for others, when you fight poverty, when you value love, when you live for change...

Then God is happening in time and space.

The time is now. It is our time. The space is the reality we live within each day.

God is happening.

Life will be more everything.

It is Christmas all over again.

CHAPTER 3

Light in Darkness

Let's Light Up the Dark!

I HAVE FOUR WREATHS on the front of my house. Three are hanging from the railing on my porch and the fourth graces my front screen door. From sunset and for the next six hours there are two spotlights that light up the wreaths and the entire front of the house.

The house is brighter now than it is in the middle of the summer!

It is our custom and tradition this time of the year to light up so many things, houses, trees, bushes, businesses, light poles, even (ugly) sweaters. Basically, we don't like the elongated darkness that surrounds us during these darkest days of the year.

The lights are bright and their colors add so much to a black, grey, and white time of the year.

The positioning of Christmas on 12/25 has everything to do with light in this dark time of the year. In ancient days, the Roman people had a Great Feast on or about December 25. They called it the feast of the "Unconquerable Sun." And they celebrated (what many still do today) the winter solstice. They celebrated the "Return of the Sun." The sun was beginning to return to the northern sky, and more light would be added every day.

Once the Winter Solstice occurs, the days get longer (too slowly for me)! The earth will warm and thaw. The seeds will be planted. The crops will grow. We will eat, and life will continue for one more year. And it begins with the Return of the Sun.

Can you see where this is going?

On or about 12/25 in those days, a much smaller group of people called Christians began a counter-culture celebration of their own. (And eventually, it blew the other one away!) They began the celebration of "The Return of the Son."

What do you need to be alive? The Sun; we will have food.

What do you need to be alive? The Son; we will have food: The Body of Christ.

The earliest celebration of Christmas was not the Christ event in Bethlehem, but the return of Christ in glory. So many spiritual traditions are built on the cultural and historic traditions of their times. There is a wise saying: grace builds on nature.

So let's light up the dark. String lights -- lots of lights! Let's make it festive, with a great feast and celebration!

"I am the light of the world. Whoever follows me will never walk in darkness."

"The light shines in the darkness, and the darkness has not overcome it."

We will be filled with love and hope because *"God so loved the world that he sent his only son..."*

You need the sun to survive? We need the Son to survive.

It is the time of the year when we hear about so many acts of generosity and care for those less fortunate people. And we choose to participate with our gifts of time, treasure and talent to assist other people. The activity of God, through us, is breaking through the routine of life to make it better for all.

There is a three word-mantra used among Christian people these dark days before Christmas: Come, Lord Jesus!

So, let us turn on the lights; let's sing the songs of the season; let's share the light with those in need; let's be humbled by all the blessing we have received.

And let's sing, chant, and say "Merry Christmas" to everyone...because a Light shines in the darkness, and the darkness will not overcome it!

The People in Darkness Have Seen a Great Light

THE FIRST THING I do is reach for the switch. Otherwise, there's no focus or balance. No dimension or perspective. But just hit that switch. Like magic, immediately, it is all so different. It's a good feeling, very re-assuring.

With the flip of a switch, from darkness to light, you see it the way it really is. No guessing or risk taking. It is right there: in front of you, on both sides, above, underneath, behind you, too.

We see life with the flip of a switch. With light we see life all around us, just as it is. For better or worse.

It is a light shining in darkness. The drama is in the contrast. From dark to light, nothing to something. From vagueness to clarity, confusion to certitude.

It is that contrast that dominates Christmas. The religious story as well as the secular season. In a world of extra-long nights, seemingly devoid of natural color, of extra-long nights, seemingly devoid of natural color, colorful lights and bright ornaments are hopeful reminders of what is to come.

We are more. We are destined to live in light. Our future is bright. Life is filled with hope. That is our religious story, too.

Isaiah says, *"The people in darkness have seen a great light."*

John says, *"The Light shines in the darkness and the darkness did not overcome it."*

We name our Light: Savior, Emmanuel, Christ.

And, just like the bright lights in the winter darkness, the drama of our religious story is in the contrast. Christ lights a way out of darkness: a Divine Intervention that gives perspective and balance, dimension and focus, just like the flip of that switch.

We can see so clearly now that we can actually "see" what can be.

The revelation of Christ lights our way out of darkness, that godless place of hard hearts, fear, despair and powers of violence. The darkness can be the subtleness of indifference, the possession by painful memories, or the slavery of deep-seated angers.

The contrast is dramatic: *"Do not fear, Mary. You have found favor with God."*

From fear to favor: *"He shall be called Emmanuel,*

a name which means God is with us." Aloneness to Presence.

"They prostrated themselves and did him homage."
Wisdom worships Hope.

We Observed
His Star at its Rising...

IT'S DARK!

That can describe so much.

Tonight beyond these walls, it is dark. It is also that time of the year: late December, a dark time of the year.

Yet "It's dark" is descriptive of life beyond time and season. There is darkness in our lives when life's struggles overtake us. So many people live in darkness: victims of ignorance, grief, illiteracy, prejudice, hate, sickness, violence, persecution, war.

It is in the dark where evil lurks, bad deeds are done, shady characters live.

Yet, there is more. It is in the stark darkness, and the darker the better, that light can be seen and appreciated.

"We observed his star at its rising..."

It had to be dark to see that. And that darkness is descriptive of life beyond time and season.

The Savior's star, the Messiah's light, is seen and appreciated best up against life's darkness.

The child is light for those who live in darkness.

The child is hope for those who live in fear.

The child is communion for those who live in isolation.

The child is truth for those who live the lie.

The child is healing for those who live in pain.

The child is love for those who live with hate.

Yet, there are times when the darkness seems to overtake the light: when vengeance is rewarded. When grudge takes the upper hand. When violence undermines respect. When war kills the love.

But as dark as it gets personally or socially, as dark as it becomes inside and out, remember the Tradition: *"We observed his star at its rising. The light shines in the darkness, and the darkness did not overcome it."*

As a matter of fact, it is bright out there!

We Have Come to Do Him Homage

STARS ARE AMAZING. They are so far away.

Except for the sun, we can only see stars in the dark. The darker it is, the brighter stars appear to be.

Such a contrast: dark and light.

The Christmas Child was revealed by a star. In the darkness of life a new star, a new light shined brightly.

Funny thing, though, not everybody saw it.

Did you ever wonder why?

All we need to do is look and there it is. That's it. The light of the star is there for all to see.

But you have to look.

The Christmas child, like light in darkness, is there for all to see.

But like the Wise Ones from the East, we must be looking for something. In those dark places in our lives, can we search for Light?

Can we see a Presence, pushing through the darkness, showing us a path to peace?

Can we see a Presence, wrapped in love, that allows us to overcome grudges and embarrassments?

Can we see a Presence, as food for all, who will fill us up and pour love, care and life into others?

The Christmas Star reveals a choice: light or dark. Live as we are or reach for the stars and be fully alive.

May we pay homage to the Child of Light. May we, in turn, radiate His star's light, to all who cross our path.

Merry Christmas.

Seeing His Star
Christmas, 2020

BOY OH BOY, do I need to see His star this year!

The Magi told King Herod that they saw *"His star rising in the East, and we have come to worship him."*

Was there a real star, His star, rising in the East? I don't think that is the point. Stars in religious and secular literature are more important symbolically than any other way.

But in this narrative from the Gospel of Matthew, the most important word is "His."

In the ancient world, people were assigned a star to signify their prominence as a King, a Queen, a Caesar, a Seer, a General, a Patriarch.

A child born in Bethlehem has his own star? No way! Stars were "assigned" to those with power and influence.

And I need His star this year, this Christmas season. We have seen and experienced so much darkness this year...

Fighting an enemy that we cannot see...

Living among economic brokenness...

Looking for truth in the midst of "distortions"...

Not knowing where life will take us.

Dr. King knew that well, *"Darkness cannot drive out darkness, only light can do that."*

Ending a year with such darkness, we need the light from "His" star.

This Christmas may we pause and open our eyes, our spiritual eyes, to see the light coming from His star, that no form of darkness can overcome.

CHAPTER 4

The Story

The Program

THE PLAYERS
Two Kings (Roman Emperor, New Born King)
Gabriel
Shepherds
Animals
Carpenter
Pregnant Mother
Magi
Heavenly Hosts
Chief Priests
Scribes
Quirinius
Angels
Savior

THE PROPS
Stable
The East
Swaddling Clothes
Gold
Frankincense

Myrrh
Star
Manger
Fields
Bethlehem
Judea
Jerusalem
Inn

THE THEOLOGICAL SYNOPSIS

"In the beginning was the Word, and the Word was with God, and the Word was God."

What came to be through Him was life, and this life was the Light of the human race. The true Light which enlightens everyone was coming into the world.

"And the Word became flesh and made his dwelling among us."

And we saw his glory, the glory as of the Father's only Son.

THE HUMAN STORY

When the time came for her to have her child, she gave birth to her first-born son. *"She wrapped him in swaddling clothes and laid him in a manger."*

"Today in the city of David a Savior has been born for you who is Messiah and Lord. Glory to God in the highest, and on earth peace to those on whom his favor rests."

THE GREETING

Merry Christmas!

"Wow!"

THE REACTIONS are almost always positive and up-lifting: "Wow! Isn't that cute?! Very pretty. Amazing! Wonderful!"

They are reactions to the many different ways the "Christmas Story" is portrayed and communicated... from children's pageants to musical renditions with casts of thousands.

After all, the story has all the elements of a great production...angels singing, shepherds in fear and awe, magi with some great gifts dressed to the nines, a moving star, a wicked king, an announcement of peace, a caring husband, a loving mom and a cute little baby named Jesus, Messiah, Emmanuel and Savior.

Wow!

However, wow and amazement are not the called for reactions to this Good News. Though sincere, those reactions do little more than titillate the observers.

True wonder and amazement must be internalized by us.

What we see is a drama taking place in word or pageant.

What we realize is that the Good News of the Christmas Story and all its wonder is taking place within us.

In every age and every Christmas, we must become aware of a spiritual process going on within us to bring forth Christ into the world.

The rhetoric of war must be countered by our living a messianic mission of peace. The alienation and bitterness toward people will be overcome by the love we birth to others in God's name.

To people who can react with a "wow" to pomp and pageant... but remain lonely and so spiritually hungry, we will take the bread for the world found lying in a manger into ourselves. May His food and drink become life and love for them all. Imagine the amazement when we pull that off!

Wow!

You Have Found Favor with God

PROBABLY MORE THAN ANY OTHER STORY we have every heard, the Christmas story has had a significant impact on us. Can we ever remember a time when we didn't know the story?

Probably not.

Our minds know every detail, probably in color and 3-D, too...the imagery is almost beyond description:

Angels appearing and singing. A moving, mysterious star. A virgin mother. A fearful king. Astrologers bearing gifts. A Child born in a stable.

But even more than the imagery, we know the significance of that story better than any other, too.

Because people were faithful to what they believed to be the plan of God in the world, their God was given "birth." No longer was their God a promise to be fulfilled or a story to be told, but for the faithful people in the Christmas Story, the God of Promise was one with them and one of them.

Their faithfulness to what they believed was the

very best way to live. It allowed a God to break through their lives in a dramatic way.

Emmanuel: God is with us.

Because we know the Christmas story so well, we know the part that each of the people in the story played.

It's our turn now. We must live our part of the Christmas story. How is Emmanuel, the God-with-us, being born among us today?

The God of the Christmas story who visited Mary, Joseph, shepherds, and wise men in a very special way, pushes into our lives today.

It is Christmas!

Let us show the world how.

They Were Very Much Afraid

ISN'T IT INTERESTING just how frightening good news can be?

You finally get the promotion, and you immediately worry if you can do a good job. In the midst of falling in love, you worry if it will really last. You find yourself pregnant...at last! But will the baby be healthy?

And there is the story of the girl born blind. The genius of medical science gave her the gift of sight. When the bandages were removed, she opened her eyes to see.

She quickly closed them tight. She grabbed the comfort of the dark for fear of the light.

The journey of life for each of us is the constant tension between fear and love, between fright and risk.

That is the Christmas story.

In the Gospel of Luke, we read about four Annunciations of the coming of the Christ, and each was met with a reaction of fear. But one had a response unlike the other three.

The Angel Gabriel says to Mary, *"You have found favor with God. You will conceive and give birth a son, who will be called Jesus. He will be great and called Son of the Most-High."* But Mary was greatly troubled by Gabriel's words.

Joseph hears in a dream, *"Joseph, do not be afraid to take Mary as your wife."*

To the shepherds in the field, *"An angel of the Lord appeared to them, and the glory of the Lord shone round them, and they were filled with great fear."*

The fourth is to King Herod by the Magi. *"Where is the new-born king of the Jews? We have come to worship him. When Herod the king heard these things, he was troubled and all Jerusalem with him."*

Fear is common to all this Good News. The first three reactions to this announcement went from fear to trust, belief and love. They encountered the fullness of life. They encountered God.

One, King Herod, did not trust the Good News. Holding on to his fear, he ordered the death of all the little children. By doing so, he brought more violence, sadness, and death into the world.

The strategy here is this: fear constrains; love releases.

Fear is commonplace in each of our lives. It can hold us back from experiencing a lot of new things and new possibilities. It can hold us back from being more fully alive. But in the middle of the fear within us, there also exists risk, courage and love needed to let go and to trust. But we must decide what direction we will take and what strategy we will use.

Today we are those who experience annunciations. We are the Mary's, the Joseph's, the shepherds and the Herod's. Each one of us must choose: love or fear; trust or fright.

Mary, Joseph, and the shepherds said yes to the unknown. They let go and let God. Herod did not. He did not let go. He did not let God. He killed the little children.

Can we let go? Can we let God?

Can we say, *"Be it done to me according to your will?"*

Can we listen to the deep spirit within us when possibilities are presented to us?

Can we take a risk and say yes to love, and say no to selfishness?

Come, Lord Jesus, come.

CHAPTER 5

The Manger

Food for the World

As I LOOK UP right now from where I sit and type, I can see my manger inside my Christmas crib. It is small (big enough for my tiny baby). It has hay on its bottom (no blanket). The baby is wrapped tightly (swaddling clothes) with his arms reaching up and out toward me! The manger rests in a stable (no hospital or birthing room). Mom and Dad are on either side of their child's manger.

That manger was a feeding trough for animals. They came to a manger to feed. In fact, in French the word "manger" literally means "to eat."

"Here, take and eat. This is my body given for you."

I read so much into that little painted plaster baby:

"Come to me all you who are weary and burdened..."

"I myself am the bread of life."

"Those who come to me shall not hunger."

"He was known to them in 'the breaking of bread.'"

"He gave thanks and broke the loaves. They all ate and were satisfied."

Keep in mind the Gospels were written in reverse order. They began with the death and resurrection of Jesus, worked their way through the words and actions of Jesus as he journeyed through Galilee. Lastly the gospels of Luke and Matthew focused on the birth of Jesus.

Jesus is depicted as feeding people so many times and so many ways throughout the Gospel texts. He was feeding them forgiveness, life itself, sight, healing, and abundance (loaves and fishes).

Is it any wonder then that he is placed in a manger? From the very beginning he is revealed for who he is and will be in his life - food for others, the bread of life, food for the world.

From the manger to the altar of the Lord: *"Take and eat. This is my body given for you."*

We need only to utter a single word.

Amen.

Swaddling Clothes

SO MUCH OF MY understanding of the Christmas Story came to me when I was a child.

I cannot remember a time when I did not know the story of the birth of Christ. I am quite certain that my mom and dad told me that story every Christmas - way before I could ever appreciate the story or understand the words.

The imagery in the story is really made for the imagination of kids: a birth of a baby in a manger, three wise men, a star rising in the East, a king, shepherds and sheep, a Caesar, no room in the inn. The imagination of a child can draw an amazing picture.

All this imagery of Joseph and Mary and the baby created a picture within me of poverty—a couple who had no place to stay, birthing a child in a stable, and wrapping that newborn in swaddling clothes.

I always imagined those swaddling clothes were rags found in the stable. Poor people made do with what they had and what they could find.

On the contrary. Swaddling clothes were not a symbol of poverty; swaddling clothes were a symbol of love.

According to the scripture, King Solomon at birth was wrapped in swaddling clothes. He was wrapped in love and privilege. So was the child lying in the manger.

So were we.

I never get tired of seeing on facebook and other platforms a new-born wrapped tightly in a hospital blanket. I call that blanket swaddling clothes. I am always reminded of the Christ Child. I see love. I see hope. I cannot help but smile. And I wonder what that tiniest child will become someday.

My smile comes from deep within. I see the cycle of life, beginning again in the youngest and littlest human being. Someone has arrived, I pray, who can make it better than we have.

What I thought was a sign of poverty when I was growing up, those swaddling clothes, has become symbolic of the unlimited possibilities within us. Those swaddling clothes tell me how wealthy I really am.

We may be experiencing a poverty of riches, or clout, or maybe even a poverty of opportunity. But there is no poverty of blessings and blessedness. As a matter of fact, we have an abundance of blessings and blessedness.

In each of our lives there is no poverty of love pouring into us. We are the recipients of an abundance of love. When we begin to think otherwise, turn to the Christmas Story. Read it again.

God so loved the world that he wraps God's children in love

We have been wrapped that way, too. We are a part of the family.

Away In a Manger

IT WAS EMPTY. As a matter of fact, it was always empty.

It had never been used before. It was designed and built for something that was yet to come.

I saw it in what was to be the baby's room. Yet, there was no baby. But even then, it had a mysterious aura about it.

I returned two weeks later. This time it was full.

In its middle was the littlest of children, wrapped tight, head to the side, eyes closed, fast asleep.

It's still had a mysterious aura for me.

What in our culture is called a crib, a common resting place for the new-born, at another time was given the name manger—an uncommon resting place for a new-born.

A crib was a place to sleep and grow and be watched over by the givers of love and nurturers of life. A manger is a place from which animals were nurtured and fed.

It was about to be used again, so says the story.

This time it would be filled by the mystery of the birth of a child. From this manger the child's destiny would be revealed: to be food for those who hunger, to be life for those who were weak.

And so from the very beginning, they were told they would find a Child in that manger wrapped in swaddling clothes. The experience continues to this day of recognizing Him in the breaking of bread. He was then and continues to be now...life for the world.

To acknowledge the presence of the Lord in our midst is not so much to point to a historical reality, but to live out a spiritual truth.

We acknowledge and call the Anointed One our Lord of Life. Because we, who have received food and life from Him, will be food and life for one another because of Him.

That's what it is all about. *Away in a manger...* you will find a Child wrapped in love.

And within us, who dare to use the name of the Child, you will find the spirit of the Child, as we go forth giving food and life to all.

No Room in the Inn

LIFE IS CRUEL. To protect ourselves we take some interesting precautions.

Precious items and important documents are locked in vaults. Caller ID screens our telephone calls. Motion sensors trigger alarms and lights. Passwords shield us from predators. Car doors lock automatically. We live peacefully behind strong doors, alarmed windows, and deadbolts.

That's life. Don't take risks. It's tough out there. How cruel can life get?

As a kid, I always got angry and mad when I heard that line in the Christmas Story that Joseph and Mary were turned away from the Inn because there was no room.

Talk about cruelty! You mean that innkeeper couldn't find some small space for a woman to birth her child? Give me a break! Throw somebody out! The woman is about to give birth, for God's sake. Make room!

I think back now—my South Side Chicago roots were talking for me. That Inn Keeper needed an "attitude adjustment!" That could be arranged.

But as I grew, I have another take on the no-room-in-inn experience.

What is an Inn? A hotel, motel, a place for overnight lodging. Who stays in an Inn? Travelers, people on vacation, business people.

There was "No room in the Inn" because the Christ Child about to be born did not fit the profile. I believe this was a magnificent rendering of simple spiritual significance: "Today in the town of David, a Savior has been born to you."

He was of the House of David. He was not a traveler on his way to a permanent location. He was born where he would live: in, with, and among God's people. The Child Jesus was home. Not a foreigner; not distant from others; not on a journey to some other place. He is, was and always will be Emmanuel, God-With-Us.

And in that manger—a "feeding trough" in Isaiah —that Child would be food for the world!

As my journey through life continues, I've discovered that Gospel narratives were not simply of times past. They were written for us, too. We need to find ourselves in the stories.

No Room in the Inn? Could we be the Inn Keeper? Is that us in this birth narrative of the Christ?

If so, then you and I must make room. Make room in your heart. Get some other stuff out of the way in order to do that. Open some room in your soul.

And more than that. Embrace what needs to find room in your Inn. Right before us is the Divine Presence seeking a place to be born and a place to dwell.

Once we make room and open those Inn doors to allow that Divine Presence a place to dwell, then please do not lock those doors.

The Divine Presence, Emmanuel, God-With-Us, is not a personal possession or a seasonal gift just for you and me. It is our time in human history to write (and live) a different ending to this part of the ancient story.

If we choose to make room and allow Emmanuel, God to dwell with us, then just like Joseph and Mary, we are the Christ-bearers. We will go from door to door and Inn to Inn seeking other places for Emmanuel, that Divine Presence, to dwell.

To those locked behind doors of racial, sexual, gender, religious, or age discrimination, we will seek room to allow the genuine and gentle respect for all humanity to find place in them. We will seek to replace human hatred with Divine respect, to replace prejudice with insight, and to replace so much rage with the everlasting peace of the Lord.

To the perpetrators of so much violence—from

ISIS to North Lawndale to Kenosha and beyond—we will pray that a more hopeful and peaceful way of life will find room in the Inns of the world.

And for each one of us, as we open those doors ever so slightly, we will work hard to allow Emmanuel, the God that dwells with us, to silence our sharp tongues, our rash judgments and our prejudices; to calm our fears and diminish our occasional angers.

No room in the Inn? Think about it. At this time in the history of the world, it is our time and our task to *make room* for the way of the Lord.

He dwells with us.

He is not leaving. We may take it for granted too often. We might even try to leave. And we can leave for a period of time, or forever. But He doesn't.

He dwells with us.

Personally, I am comforted by that, and challenged by that. Is my conduct and behavior welcoming and warm? Do the actions of my life reveal the One who dwells with me?

Yes. There can always be room in the Inn.

He dwells with us.

CHAPTER 6

The Child

One Tiny Child Can
Change the World

I BELIEVE IT. I always have.

No one ever birthed just a child.

They have given life to a saint.

Behold, a new human being has arrived on the face of the earth. Male or female, makes no difference. There is the child - fresh from the womb, totally innocent, absolute potential.

Look! A human being who has done nothing wrong and who incarnates all human possibility. That sounds like a saint to me.

I cannot possibly imagine what the experience must be like in mind or body for a mother, who birthed a human being, to have her child placed in her arms for the first time.

"She gave birth to her first born and wrapped him in swaddling clothes."

The heart that beat within her is now beating outside of her in rhythm to her own. And to imagine that little heart in this world might possibly beat for a hundred years.

She holds her child with such delicacy as if the baby might break.

I treasure this picture of my mom holding me like that. I can see the look in her eyes and try to imagine the dreams she might have for the package of love she is holding.

Yep. It's more than a new baby. It's a saint! A human being at that moment with limitless possibilities, talents and skills. "My child can do everything!" It seems to me that is the dream and conviction of every parent at the moment of birth.

That scene is what makes Christmas so special. That scene never grows old. *"God so loved the world that God sent His son..."*

Ah, the child, that little package of innocent love. And guess who that was at one time in human history? It was you. It was me. "Mom" and "Dad" are titles limited to certain people. Child, newborn, son, daughter, little package of love are some of the titles that belong to every human being at one time. Totally Innocent, complete potential, saint. Yep, that was us.

"You are my son. You are my daughter. This day I have begotten you." We may or may not be the father or the mother, but we all are the child...all grown up.

The wonder of Christmas for me is always the

Child, the littlest, the most innocent, of human beings.

I invite us to fix our eyes on a crèche scene this Christmas. Don't be in a hurry. Stare at it for a while. Let your eyes move from the dad to the mom and back again.

And then focus your attention for a while on the child wrapped in those swaddling clothes. If you look long and hard enough, can you begin to see what you and I looked like at one time?

May that Child, born to that mom and dad, once again this year refresh our own potential. Staring at who we once were, in that Child's name, may we recommit ourselves to bring life to others.

And like that Child, may we look up, reach for the stars and be a bearer of the light of the world to all.

"One tiny child can change the world. One shining light can show the way." – *Melissa Manchester*

Give Life to the World

THERE IS PRACTICALLY universal agreement: it's a life-altering experience.

Afterwards, you look at life so differently. Almost every decision from then on is influenced by what happened.

It must be experienced first-hand. Print, text, video or audio just won't suffice. Neither will second-hand knowledge.

It must happen to you and by you.

It is the experience which *is* Christmas.

"The days of her confinement were completed. She gave birth to her first-born son and wrapped him in swaddling clothes."

The drama of dramas: to give life to the world!

It's true isn't it? From that moment on, so much of life—every waking moment—is viewed through that birthed new life. Women and men, moms and dads, now see everything through what they have created.

Mary birthed new life to the world: a divine life.

That's the Christmas Story, the Christmas Mystery. Yet, the Mystery of Christmas is not exclusive to Mary. It is not even relegated to an historical moment.

It is what happens to all those faithful ones, to those who believe that a Divine Presence can have life through them. We can birth in this world love or hate, life or death, freedom or pain, hope or despair.

Isn't it true?

When we give life to the very best, the Christmas Mystery continues.

You, too, can give life to the world: Divine Life.

So, it's your time in human history.

Give life to God.

She Gave Birth
to her First-Born Son

I AM A FIRST-BORN.

How about you?

Where do you fit in your family birth-order? Birth order is trendy these days. Some would say that where we fit in our family birth order reveals some of our traits and behavior patterns.

We are told that the first-born is in charge, the leader, the boss, and, also, the first recipient of parental rewards and punishments (as the others look on!)

The middle child must try a bit harder for attention.

The last-born can be easy-going, learning from the older ones. The last-born can watch the sibs and find out what rings a parent's bell and what they like to see in their kids. That last-born hears the constant comments from the older ones..."You got it made. They treat you so much better than they ever treated us!"

I am also the last-born! I am the beginning and the end!

Like Jesus I am an only child.

Yet the birth story of Jesus in the Gospel of Luke is hinting at another understanding of birth order.

We are told that Mary gave birth to her first-born son and laid him in a manger. In spiritual literature calling someone a first-born is to signal others are still to come.

You mean Jesus had sibs? In a very special way, yes.

"First-born" in the birth story in Luke's Gospel alludes to a future time when others will receive the revelation of Jesus and live as He did.

That future time is now—this Christmas.

We are the ones who have been invited into that family.

We, too, are sons and daughters of God. We, too, are brothers and sisters of the Lord Jesus.

Where we are positioned in that birth order has only one significance. We are a family following the leadership of the first-born. We have been given the revelation. We have been blessed with that faith.

Like a middle child, we will try hard to live a life of grace, forgiveness, compassion and living for others.

Like a last-born, we have countless heroes, mentors, and saints from whom to learn.

But we will be most like a "first-born."

We will invite others to follow the example of the life of Emmanuel – God-With-Us, into a full communion with all humankind, into a peace beyond anger and violence, and into a life that knows no end.

That's not a bad family of which to be a part, is it?

The Real Christmas Spirit

I HAVE OVERHEARD PEOPLE commenting about the *real* Christmas Spirit. Often it is spoken as a critique of experiences that are not the "real" Spirit of the Season.

The gifts we want. The money we spend. The glitz and glitter. The secularity of a sacred religious feast.

Sometimes we are told the *real* Christmas spirit is seen as a nativity pageant with live animals and a festive choir singing religious Christmas hymns.

Really?

Others are quick to say that the *real* Christmas Spirit happens by...

Dropping coins in red kettles. A generosity so that no one goes hungry. Wrapping a coat around the arms of one who is cold. Filling food banks with abundance. Forgiving and forgetting. Peace as a replacement for terror.

Is that it?

Are those experiences the *real* Christmas spirit?

Those elements are powerful, but the *real* Christmas Spirit might be something more.

Let's consult the Tradition...

Mary "gave birth to her first-born." It alludes to a second, and maybe a third and fourth born. It alludes to a future time when others will receive the revelation of Jesus and live as he did.

Might that be you? Might that be me? The activity of the Divine is with us, too. We are part of a new family of followers, if we so choose.

"Wrapped in swaddling clothes and lying in a manger."

Wrapped in swaddling clothes reveals an intimate and loving relationship with God.

They are the two great signs that symbolize the identity and mission of the beloved Child. Ezekiel tells us that the unloved child is not wrapped in cloths. But the beloved child is washed and clothed. Jesus' belovedness is a constant theme.

"This is my son, my beloved, listen to him."

It is a relationship of everyone in the "family." His manger is a feeding trough—a sign of his mission: being food for others as a way of putting his spirit into them. It's a divine desire to be connected to the human family and for those in the family to reach out to one another.

No one is out. All are called to this full life.

Well, that's it. That's the real Christmas Spirit.

You've got it... Now give it away.

Wonder-Counselor, Mighty God

THE CHRISTMAS CHILD has been given many titles: Wonder-Counselor, Mighty God, Prince of Peace, Messiah, Son of Man, Lord of All, Light of Light, King, Ruler, Judge, True God from True God, Son of God.

Titles are earned.

How did this Christmas Child get to be called so many things?

By living life, a human life. A life just like us. *"One like us in all things but sin,"* says the scripture.

How did the Christmas Child live?

With all the powers of the gods? With all the might of kings? With all the force of judges? With all the splendor of princes?

"Tell them what you see and hear.
The blind see;
The lame walk;
The poor have good news preached to them."

That's the story of the Christmas Child. That's

the Wonder-Counselor, the Mighty God, the Prince of Peace, the Lord.

Look for the Lord where the Lord is always found: where life changes.

Seek the Wonder-Counselor in moments of compassion.

Find the Mighty God in times of forgiveness.

Discover the Prince of Peace in the good news of a just life.

Reveal the Christmas Child where you can heal, listen and care for all.

They Found the Child...

I SAW IT AGAIN TODAY.

It has nothing to do with the season of the year. As a matter of fact, it is observable every day of the year in every country on the face of the earth.

You were a part of it once and might have participated again or several times later in life.

And as often as you see it, it never grows old. It never becomes routine. It always seems new, because it is.

Not only do we see it, we are often drawn to it. We want a better look. And you cannot help but smile.

Often you speak some very spontaneous words of good and hopeful wishes. You find yourself speaking to the contents of a car seat or stroller, to a sling or a papoose device.

You are staring at the smallest human...and the most vulnerable.

For all your wisdom, talent, and skill you become momentarily fascinated with a person who can do little more than cry, wet and sleep.

Yet it is not what this little human can do or not do at the moment that draws you close, but what he or she will be able to do one day.

"The hopes and fears of all the years are met in thee tonight."

Like Magi of old, you have come upon a child.

And your gazing and staring might quickly become a pondering of all the many wonderful things the child might accomplish.

"They saw the Child with Mary, his mother."

It is always an incredible sight, isn't it?

Then and now, it is the wonder of Christmas.

Emmanuel – God-With-Us.

Our reminder of it is constant and continual.

The baby in the stroller; the Child in the manger.

We are always drawn to the presence of love, to the presence of Emmanuel—God-With-Us.

"The light shines in the darkness, and the darkness has not overcome it." – The Gospel of John

"For Today in David's City a Savior Has Been Born for You..."

SO MUCH OF EVERYONE'S LIFE has yet to be lived.

My ninety-something mother always wished that she could snow ski. Politicians thrive on assuring citizens about what can be.

One of the great problems of social and economic poverty is that it is a life filled with empty promises. Nothing ever changes.

There is a longing in the human heart for what can be—love, fulfillment, success, happiness. It is more of a constant longing than an experienced reality. It is a world of hope—a looking forward to what can be.

It is the possibility of something more. Yet so often it is just a little out of reach, always ahead of us. Maybe in sight, but not yet tangible.

Christmas is something very different. It is not focused only on future glory. It is not solely a remembrance of times past. The Christmas revelation is about now.

"Today in David's city a Savior has been born for you." It is the revelation of now—this very moment—today.

The time of only looking to tomorrow is over. The waiting and longing promised by politicians to prophets. What is always just a bit out-of-reach of you and me, is over.

What can be, is—the Messiah and Lord.

Humanity—your life and mine—is filled with a divine presence today, right now. Like shepherds in a field, magi under a star, a mother holding her child, we wait no longer.

Today, right now, we must take what we have been given, a Child wrapped in love, lying in a feeding trough. We will bear this Christ to a longing world—not through promises of what can be...someday.

But today, right now, we bear Christ, we wish Christ and we offer Christ to a world in waiting—a world that is always waiting.

The wait is over.

CHAPTER 7

Peace on Earth

The Daily Mirror

CERTIFIED CIRCULATION LARGER THAN ANY OTHER DAILY NEWSPAPER IN THE WORLD

AN HISTORIC GROUP : BRITISH AND GERMAN SOLDIERS PHOTOGRAPHED TOGETHER.

WHY DELAY?

THE DAILY MIRROR OVERSEAS WEEKLY EDITION contains all the Latest and Best War Pictures and News, and is therefore the Best Weekly Newspaper for your friends abroad. You can obtain it from your Newsagent for 2d. per copy. Address "Overseas Daily Mirror," 12, Whitefriars-street, London, E.C.

From famous friends on Christmas Day, when the British and Germans attempted an exhibited truce. The men left the trenches in exchange togetherness of the opposing Armies standing side by side.

Christmas Day, 1914: Along the Western Front

Out of the Trenches

IT BEGAN IN THE DARK of Christmas Eve. It began
with a song.

"*Stille Nacht, Heilige Nacht*
Alles schlaft, einsam wacht"

The other side, the enemy, replied in song.
"*Silent Night, Holy Night*
All is calm, all is bright"

A third group followed in song.
"*Douce nuit! Sante nuit!*
Dans les cieux! L'astre luit!

It was Christmas in the trenches of World War I. Men,
soldiers and enemies to each other, began singing common Christmas carols in their own language. Those
carols were a part of their lives since they were little
boys in Germany, France, England, Belgium, and the
United States. That night they discovered that they
had more in common with each other than their na-
tionalism. They had a common faith. That night they

97

all celebrated the same religious experience – the birth of Emmanuel, God-With-Us.

For some reason, scary as it was, one or two began to leave their trenches unarmed. They began to walk into "no man's land." The other side began to do the same. They allowed each other to carry away their dead. Soon after that, "enemies" began exchanging candy, cigarettes, and food rations. Their officers and commanders were incapable of stopping this.

For less than a day the ordinary soldiers stopped a world war on Christmas Eve and Christmas Day.

Why? What caused this to happen?

I have always wondered what those soldiers were thinking when they began with singing common

Christmas carols, and then found the courage to leave their safety zones.

O Holy Night. It is the night of our dear Savior's birth. Holy infant so tender and mild, sleep in heavenly peace.

How can we sing those carols and continue to do what we are doing?

Maybe the birth of the Child in Bethlehem that they read about, prayed about, wondered about and sang about all their lives was now moving them to recall that single sentence from the Gospel of Luke: "Glory to God in the highest heaven, and on earth peace to those on whom God's favor rests."

With those words rattling through your head, maybe that on Christmas Eve it made no sense to kill another human being—even one who might kill you. Who knows for sure?

Maybe they began to realize who they really were.

On Christmas Day and every day, they were more than soldiers and even more than English, American, French, Belgian, and German. They were sons of God. They were, in 1914, *"those on whom God's favor rests."*

I will never know why they started the Christmas Truce of 1914. Not a one of them is living to tell me. But they made it happen. It was the only time in recorded history that a war was halted on Christmas— even for less than a day.

But it happened. It is documented. It is real. The birth of a first-born son wrapped in love, placed in a feeding trough, because he was food for the world, was the reason that caused a World War to stop ... even for a very short time. But not only that, but also it allowed *those on whom God's favor rests* to reach out a hand, not a bayonet. They felt the common human flesh found in

Memorial to the Christmas Truce 1914,
Staffordshire, England

every human being—even in the flesh of a Child in the manger.

If it can happen on a battlefield, then it can happen in a family, in a neighborhood, in a city—anywhere. We can even embrace a person with whom we have a grudge.

In such a polarized society, we can see what can be. It is always so much more than what is.

In time when name-calling and demonizing so many among us is becoming accepted practice, we have inherited a name that is shared by all: "*You will conceive in your womb and bear a son. And you shall name him Jesus.*"

The Christmas truce only happened once. Never before. Never since. And it only happened for less than one day. But the birth of a Child did stop a war.

The remembrance of the Christ event, Emmanuel: God-With-Us, happens time and time again. And the Christmas truce testifies that Emmanuel appears in unexpected places -- like a no-mans-land where enemies shook hands and shared cigarettes and candy.

That was Christmas, 1914.

Christmas Peace

CHRISTMAS IS ALL ABOUT RELATIONSHIPS.

Maybe that's why it is such a tender and emotional time of the year.

As we look around us at Christmas, what is good, seems better. What is sad, seems empty. What is confused, is painful. What is loved, is terrific.

Each Christmas presents a personal challenge for us to treasure the relationships in our lives and to do something positive, if we can, about those situations which we know are not right.

Yet the experience and meaning of Christmas does not stop there. Christmas is also about the relationship of humanity to life itself.

Remember the setting of the Christmas story.
It was believed in those days that Caesar Augustus had brought peace to the world. Yet, in the midst of that "peaceful" world, there were angelic announcements to Mary, Joseph, astrologers and shepherds about *"Peace on earth to those on whom His favor rests."*

At a time of peace, another peace was revealed.

Christmas Peace was all about healing relationships. It was about making humanity healthy and filled with life.

It was not a peace thrust upon the world with the power of an army, or through the fear of an Emperor. It was not a peace installed on the backs of the poor. It was not a peace paid for by violence.

Christmas Peace was first announced to those on the "outside" in order to be a sign that, when life is right and truly peaceful, everyone has good news.

Christmas Peace means all humanity, even the disabled, the sick in mind or body, the lonely, those who mourn, the victims, the innocent children, the addicts, the educated, the simple, the single, the married...all are loved. Our lives are charged with the presence of God.

Humanity has been raised up. Human dignity is measured and achieved not by power, force and fear; not by wealth, looks or talent.

In David's City, life changed forever. Life is good, no matter what, no matter who.

Maybe that's why it's such a sacred time of the year.

Christmas Peace to you and to all of life!

Why is Religion So Divisive?

THAT WAS THE HEADLINE of the internet article on a news outlet's home page.

The writer used examples from today's popular culture ranging from wedding cakes to campaign rhetoric. The writer went on to comment about the meanness and judgments in people driven by their religious convictions...to the use of religion that drives a deep wedge among so many people, groups, and families today.

Yes. These are pretty ugly times, and sadly religion sometimes adds to the ugliness and societal divisions today.

But I believe it is the basic nature of religious tradition to be divisive. I prefer to call it the difference between Culture and Counter-Culture. The ways of the world and the social order is one lens to look at life: the Culture. But our faith offers another, completely different perspective: the Counter-Culture. And when religious faith works best, it proclaims to the world and calls us to believe in Counter-Culture possibilities.

Interestingly, you will find that experience of religious/spiritual Counter-Culture in the Birth of Jesus narratives in the Gospels of Luke and Matthew.

In Luke we read, "*In those days Caesar Augustus published a decree ordering a census of the whole world*." Caesar was given credit for ushering in age of peace, and for that he was given the title "Savior of the World." Yet it was a peace achieved through militancy, armies, violence and human suffering. It happens that way all too often - even today...in the Culture.

In Luke we also read of another Savior, an infant of Bethlehem, heralded by angels: "*This day in David's city a Savior has been born to you, the Messiah and Lord. Glory to God...peace on earth to those whom his favor rests.*" It's the Counter-Culture Savior.

Is the news about a Savior or a King? Well, both. In the birth narrative in Matthew's Gospel, you and I are presented with two Kings: Herod and the new-born King (Culture/Counter-Culture).

The Magi ask King Herod, "*Where is the new-born King?*" We would probably say, "King Herod, where is your replacement who has been recently born?" (That would probably not have been a good strategy, if you wanted to live a long life!)

What was the Child's Kingdom? As he grew in age, wisdom and grace, it was not of this world. He revealed it as a Kingdom of reconciliation, mercy and everlasting life.

Which King do we worship? The lure of power?

Or endless forgiveness? Culture? Or Counter-Culture?

Let's be honest. Which Savior or King do we worship? Which peace is truly life-giving? We are being called upon to choose one or the other, not to pay lip service to one and simply prefer the other—but to really choose. And I am convinced the choice is not that easy.

We could say, "Why Jesus, of course." But in reality, do we often really worship the opposite? We are Christians, but we are also surrounded by a world which can present a very different set of values.

In my humble opinion, truly making our choice lies in the understanding of peace announced at the birth of Jesus: the healing of relationships, and possibly to everlasting peace.

Just imagine what the Middle East would look like today, or the neighborhoods in urban America, or maybe within our own families...if those who "celebrate" Christmas, the Birth of Jesus, gave themselves to that experience of peace, the healing of all relationships, and didn't just pay lip service to it?

Remember the headline in the internet article: "Why Is Religion So Divisive?" Maybe a better question is, "Why is religion so Counter-Cultural?" Because it presents the world—and each one of us—with an alternate way of seeing and doing the same old things.

I call that a challenge! One that sadly, has always been divisive.

The story of Jesus is about making a decision to

follow or not. It is not about lip service as much as it is about adopting Jesus' way of living and acting each day in the world.

For me, living up to the expectations of Christ found in the Gospels (and the birth narratives of Jesus) has never been easy. The lure of the popular culture is very comfortable.

And in today's wonderful society, to take a stand on the values of Christmas found in Jesus Christ can appear as political.

"I don't want you to preach politics, Father. Preach God's word!"

That IS God's word!

It is time, as we prepare to celebrate this Christmas, for me to once again get ready to make some decisions.

Too often I worry that I worship the wrong Savior and pay homage to the wrong King. Then Christmas comes along once again, and I am invited to discover the life-giving Savior and King that I choose: whose power is found in forgiveness...and in Shalom, the healing of relationships. And again, I am presented with the opportunity to get it right.

Is it the right time for you to do the same? If we find that we are really no better than the popular culture, then maybe Christmas won't truly be "merry." But we all have a choice.

Dare I say "Merry Christmas?" You bet I do!

Divisions: Then and Now

ACCORDING TO A POLL by Suffolk University, the one thing on which Americans agree is that we are a divided nation. I hope some person or organization did not pay a lot of money to determine that result!

As much as I realize that division always has been and always will be a part of life, it's the meanness, anger, rage and alienation that accompanies division today that I abhor.

Division with civility was a great hallmark of America.

The story goes that President Ronald Reagan and Congressman Tip O'Neill could strongly disagree and be in each other's face regularly, but just as regularly when the work day wound down, they could enjoy an adult beverage together. When President Reagan was shot, Tip O'Neill knelt by the side of his hospital bed and prayed for him.

Though subtle, division was a key part of the Birth of Christ experience found in the Gospel of Luke...

"In those days a decree went out from Caesar Augustus that the whole world should be enrolled (in a census)."

Because in those days an era of peace began during his reign, Caesar Augustus was given another title: Savior of the world.

Well, well. Caesar Augustus, Savior of the world.

The Child Jesus, a Savior born to you.

Now what are we to do with these two Saviors of the World? This is apparently a moment of division. We must choose: Augustus or Jesus?

Why does the choice seem intellectually simple? But behaviorally, I am not so sure.

One reveals the here and now. The other leads the way to life that knows no end.

The "empire" of power, fame, money, status, privilege, influence, security, domination, tradition, habit, is so enticing, tempting, and rewarding. In Biblical language that is the Empire of Caesar Augustus, the Savior of the World. That is the way the world works...then and now. And I worship a lot of that world. It certainly has its perks, and they are not all bad. But they are not all there is.

You see, this birth narrative is so much more than a cutesy description of the birth of the Baby Jesus. It is about the intervention of the activity of God in daily life. That activity will be revealed in all the actions of Jesus.

The activity of God and Savior is less interested in the power of politics and finance...and more interested in the power to forgive...to respect all people as children of the same God, who offers salvation and eternal life to the world. This Savior asks followers to speak truth, act justly and honestly, and be respectful even to those with whom we disagree and experience division.

The Savior born in David's city is not a momentary commemoration that ends when the Christmas music stops, the churches empty, and the lights are put away for another year, and it becomes business as usual.

Rather, our Savior is incorporated into our lives to transform life into the vision that the activity of God has for life and for all people.

So, there are still two Saviors out there, and maybe many more. And two Kings, in Matthew's narrative.

It's your choice and mine to make. If we can say two words, I have a hunch I know the decision we are making...

"Merry Christmas."

CHAPTER 8

Gifts

The Most Wonderful Christmas

I LEARNED TODAY that there might be someone joining us for Christmas dinner whom I have never met before. I welcome that. But as quickly as I got the news, my mind was telling me that a gift will be needed.

For many of us, Christmas gifts are real objects, but sometimes their symbolic meaning is much more important than any monetary value.

I believe that the origin of Christmas gift giving has its roots in the Christmas story found in the second chapter of the Gospel of Matthew. "*Upon entering the house they (the Magi) saw the Child with Mary, his mother. They prostrated themselves and did him homage. Then they opened their treasures and offered him gifts of gold, frankincense and myrrh.*"

A big part of Christmas for me is giving gifts. It is our tradition to exchange Christmas gifts before or after dinner. I usually have an "extra" gift or two in my car just in case my family welcomes someone unexpectedly.

When I was younger, getting a Christmas present for my dad should have been very easy. A 6-pack of Schlitz and a bottle of Hiram Walker bourbon wrapped or unwrapped, and he would be very happy. Mom was different. She liked a lot of Christmas wrapped gifts (and so did I). My goal each Christmas was to shower them with wrapped gifts.

The best Christmas gift I ever gave was to my parents on Christmas Day, 1970.

I had been ordained a priest in May of that year. It was a life dream for me and for my mom and dad. They sacrificed greatly to support my dream. They stopped taking their annual summer travel vacation to pay my bills while I worked at an orphanage, earning $4 a week. (That is not a misprint: $4 a week.) The list of their sacrifices for me would take pages.

When the ceremony ended, I found my parents waiting outside the chapel. They gave me the warmest hug that I can still feel, more than 50 years later. I could feel my dad's tears on my check. It was the first time I ever saw him cry.

On that Christmas day after the last Mass, I drove home. I was always the "son-of-many-boxes." But that year I had only one gift. It was a colorfully wrapped tie box. My mother, who was the inquisitive one of the two, had a detective look on her face. After kissing and hugging my parents, I asked them to sit together on the sofa. I handed them the tie box and asked them to open it. I was soooo excited!

The contents inside the box were wrapped in tissue paper. On top of the paper I wrote a letter for them. I cannot remember the exact words of my letter, but I will never forget the spirit...

Dear Dad and Mom,

Merry Christmas!

Your support, sacrifices and love for me continues to be amazing and endless. During those five years I volunteered at Angel Guardian, you paid all my bills and I became aware that you were denying yourselves many things, including summer vacations. I am forever in your debt. With your wonderful help I fulfilled a lifelong dream on May 13th. Now I have a dream for you I want to fulfill. Inside this little box is the most special Christmas gift I could ever give you. I want you to get out of the winter weather this January with these airline tickets and hotel accommodations. I will meet you at the Miami airport. The next day we will fly to Nassau. I will stay with you for 2 nights. After that, you are on your own. I hope you will enjoy some time away and time together.

Thank you for everything you have done for me. I love you.

Your John

My dad cried for only the second time in my life. So did mom and so did their son. I was so happy. There was no greater gift.

Three days short of ten months after Christmas

Day, 1970 my dad died. The "Tie Box Christmas" was his last. And my best.

Those tickets and vouchers in the tie box were the gifts of the Magi: my parents' hard work, their prayers for me, and their tremendous sacrifices for my dream.

"They saw the young Child with Mary, His mother. They presented gifts to him: gold, frankincense, and myrrh." Along with airplane tickets, and hotel vouchers, those gifts were extra special. They were gifts from the heart.

Priceless.

To You is Born

ALTHOUGH EACH ONE could be used by nearly any-one, each gift you unwrap is for you and no one else.

Whether a snow shovel or shirt, pearls or crock pot, your name should be engraved on each gift. Your gifts are probably wrapped by now, with love. Each will be yours, bought with love with you in mind. And each has been given serious consideration.

But that's not the case for the ultimate Christmas gift. Though given in love with you in mind, it is not for you exclusively.

The Christmas gift is the Christmas Child, he is Emmanuel.

Jesus was not Mary's child or Joseph's child exclusively. He was a Child for the life of the world.

That's the message to the shepherds in the fields from the angel: "I am bringing you good news of great joy for all the people: To you a savior is born." Born to shepherds, to Mary, to Joseph, to astrologers from the east. To you, to me, to everyone.

From the very beginning until now, this Christmas ...our God is there for us, as gift for us.

More than Tonka toys and silver bracelets. The gift is always the same. It never changes.

Year after year, from God to us, and for us to give to each other...it is a child's love.

"You will find a child wrapped..."

The Child is gift. Never too grown-up to fear. The Child will be with us always. Even when the Child grows older.

The gift will do only what a child can do: reach for life. Give love. A Child who will always be life for the world.

Isn't that what you wrapped?

Isn't that what you want?

Isn't that what you give?

The gift is the only thing that matters now.

That's the great mystery and wonder of Faith, with some very important implications for us, the followers, the disciples.

If the Lord is born for us, then I must be there for you...

And you for me...

And we for them...

And them for us...

What a Christmas gift!

The God of Surprises Is at It Again!

THERE IS SOMETHING intrinsically good about being surprised.

A real surprise evokes such a sense of joy:

A surprise party, an unexpected visit, a gift, an insight, a love.

What magic can occur! What fun can be had! What a life-giving feeling!

There is also surprise to the surprise.

Have you ever witnessed the look and the joy on the face of the giver of the surprise, the party planner, the gift giver, the love initiator?

Joy meets joy. Wonders connect. And amazingly, the surprise is nearly mutual.

But surprises are fragile. I learned that one year.

I peeked.

Before Christmas, I found where my gifts were hidden. It was the only year I peeked. Never before. Never again. That Christmas was a bummer.

It was hard to fake surprise. The magic of the gift

was not there. Everything else was there: the tree, the wrapped gifts, the smiles of parents awaiting my reaction.

I realized at that Christmas that too much "knowledge" can hurt. You can't be too big or grown-up at Christmas. You can't act surprised at Christmas. You must be surprised.

And not just by gifts. Let us be surprised at the wonder of it all: *Emmanuel: God-With-Us*.

The Christmas story is the surprising God surprising daughters and sons with a gift, a love, a celebration in a most surprising way.

The surprise gift is a Child, God's Child; not a powerful king, ruler or warrior, but an innocent Child, born of a peasant woman; not a queen, princess or heiress.

The good news of the presence of the Child, God-with-us, is first shared with the bottom of the social ladder: shepherds; not senators, scholars or scientists. Imagine that! Now, isn't that a surprise!

Can you just see the joy on the face of the God of Surprises each time someone hears or encounters these experiences and is surprised (again) by the Christmas story?

It might happen when we will sense a unity to life...

That a Divine Reality loves us...no matter what.

That our efforts can make a difference.

That life is good. Not perfect, just very, very good.

That the hope we will feel at Christmas will move us forward again and again and time after time.

That *"the hopes and fears of all the years are met in Thee tonight."*

Our wonder at the meaning of it all is met by God's wonder at us.

Our joy at discovering Emmanuel, God dwelling with us in the Child never grows old. It is always such a wonderful surprise, such a wonder.

If it has been a while, surprise yourself this Christmas. Read the story again—out loud; it's the beginning of the Gospel of Luke and the Gospel of Matthew. Let the joy and wonder of it all confront you like the surprise of a gift, a party or a love.

Imagine the surprise of our God watching you become bug-eyed, joyously smiling as the story of a Child, a mom, angels, a faithful husband, astrologers looking for life, a fearful king, and shepherds with good news surprises us again this year.

It is such a joy to be surprised, isn't it? It never grows old!

When I Find the Right Gift, I Smile

WHEN I THINK the origin of gift-giving began with the Magi following a Star that led them to ask King Herod where they can find the new-born King, I smile.

"Wise men" indeed! Here they are asking the reigning King where they might find his replacement! That could cost them their lives!

But they truly were wise after all, because the star led them beyond Herod and Jerusalem to Bethlehem where they found the Child with his mother, and there they presented him with gifts: gold, frankincense, and myrrh.

These three gifts are symbols of a greater reality, more important than the gifts themselves. They reveal who they considered this new-born King to be.

The gift of Gold is a symbol of royalty.

Frankincense is a symbol of connectivity to the Divine. In the ancient world when frankincense is burned, the sweet-smelling smoke goes up into the sky (heavens). It is a symbol that the heavens (divine) and earth (humankind) are connected. The Child is known to be the son of the divine.

The difficult gift is Myrrh— a symbol of suffering. It was used for anointing, and probably was used to anoint the body of Jesus when he taken down from the cross. It says that life is hard. He will suffer and die, but he will be anointed with the sweet-smelling oil.

All are symbolic of greater realities. That's what gift-giving at Christmas is for me. I make a list for whom I will buy each gift. I try to focus on who I perceive each person to be. I search for something that speaks to that person (or maybe to something they have been experiencing during the year). The process can be long to find the right symbolic gift, but when I find it, I smile.

My gifts are all wrapped now and they are under my Christmas tree. Next I will bag them and make them ready to go with me to each location. And I must admit I get great joy in watching each of my gifts get unwrapped. Even if the recipient can't see the gift's symbolic meaning, I can. And I will smile with each one.

I think the Magi must have smiled, too.

Once opened, there is only one thing left:

Enjoy!

A Gift – Pure and Simple

SOMETHING HAS GONE WRONG.

On the surface they are called gifts, and more precisely, at this time of the year, Christmas gifts.

Though not expressed in these exact words, some have been converted into expectations. And, all too sadly, demands.

"I want you to get me this for Christmas." Our response: to purchase the specifically requested Christmas gift. In return we will receive a genuine thanks, maybe a hug and kiss, and perhaps a note expressing sincere, honest appreciation.

Yet in many ways that was not a gift given nor received. Gifts cannot be demanded—even subtly. A real gift is a surprise of joy, straight from the heart of the giver. A gift is always an unexpected encounter, experience, or moment.

Christmas is filled with gifts – pure and simple. Not asked for—but freely given.

"God so loved the world that in the fullness of time, God sent a Son..."

"Mary, you have found favor with God. You will bear a son."

"Fear not, shepherds, a savior has been born to you and to all the people, the Messiah and Lord."

Now that is a gift! No demand and never an expectation. And the greatest of all gifts usually are life-changing moments.

That is why Christmas is gift—pure and simple.

In spite of all the joys and sorrows, the hopes and disappointments, the broken hearts and overflowing ones, we are given Christmas.

We gather around this great gift of Divine Love to us and to all the world, incarnate in a Child, and dwelling with each one of us, too.

If you think about, if you ponder it in your heart, the only response is words of genuine thanks, actions that reveal the love of the Giver and, on a special day like this...

With a mind filled with a dream about what life can be...

And a heart overwhelmed with the realization that we can be so loved...

And the courage to make this unexpected gift a way of life...

The only appropriate response is a wide-eyed, full-face smile and a...

"Merry Christmas!"

CHAPTER 9

Tis: the Season
Take Care of Some People

Life in the Season of Giving

HE GRABBED MY HAND to shake it, as he always did when leaving Mass. But this time, several weeks before Christmas, there was something in the palm of his right hand. I took it and put it in my right rear pocket without knowing what it was. He looked at me as he shook my hand, and said, "Take care of some people."

A few minutes later I discovered 5 one hundred dollars bills in that pocket. "Take care of some people."

About five years later, a woman dashed into Church one Sunday. "Our son is in the car while my husband parks it. I just want to give you a heads-up. Our son was confirmed recently. He wants to give you the money he received in gifts for his Confirmation."

He soon arrived. Reaching out to shake my hand, I could see he held a folded envelope that he pushed into my hand. "Take care of some people," he said.

OMG! He listened! He must have been in about in second or third grade when he heard that line spoken during a homily. But it stuck. Now with about $37 in an envelope he wanted me to do what the man coming out of church did. He wanted me to take his Confirmation cash and "Take care of some people."

But it wasn't the Christmas season. It was the spring season.

That seems to be the point. Taking care of some people is not seasonal.

We are told that Christmas is a season of giving. I beg to differ. Life is the season of giving. Poor people need to be fed, clothed, housed, and receive medical attention in July, too.

As we inch closer to Christmas and beyond, I have an idea. How about we take a coffee can (remember those?), or a beer pint glass, a flowerpot, a vase, a fishbowl, a water pitcher...whatever can hold a bunch of paper money (a little at a time). Then let's add these words: "Take Care of Some People." Tape that to our "bank." Let's add one single dollar a day until next Christmas season.

Let's make this project our reminder that from this "season of giving" until the next, every day— a dollar-at-time—is our life of giving. Maybe that's what it means to be driven by our faith.

"*She gave birth to her first-born son and laid him in manger.*"

A manger was a feeding trough for animals. It is place where animals came to be fed. From the beginning the Child Jesus was food for others. In other words, "Take care of some people."

What a great way to clear out your "bank" during the Christmas season: Take Care of Some People.

Merry Christmas, Dan

BACK IN THE MID-1970S, most Tuesdays after school I would drive a van full of our high school kids down into the bowels of Chicago to the headquarters of Catholic Charities at 126 N. Desplaines Street. In the alley behind the rear of the six story building at 5:30 every evening Catholic Charities provided hot soup and bread to over 200 homeless and alcoholic men who lived in what was called "Skid Row."

Under the direction of Deacon Pete, our kids would work the soup and bread line, serving the men until all had their fill. Then we would return to the suburbs. It was a good learning experience for our parish's high school kids. They came into contact with human beings who were near the bottom of society's ladder. They witnessed where they lived. It was one of the most depressing, run-down neighborhoods in Chicago. In those days you would be hard pressed to find anybody or anything hopeful or positive on Skid Row.

Dan was one of our kids. When he was in college,

he began returning to Skid Row each Christmas Eve. His car was loaded with as many Christmas trees as he could stuff into it and on top of it. Dan would approach a Christmas tree lot when it was getting ready to close on Christmas Eve and close for the season. He told the people who ran the lot that he was looking for some trees he could bring down to Catholic Charities on Skid Row to add some Christmas spirit to such a depressing place. Obviously, he was looking for a deal. They gave him some of their leftover trees.

In the dark and cold of Christmas Eve, Dan drove the trees down to Skid Row. The next morning, Christmas Day, there would be a nice buffet meal at a union hall a block away from Catholic Charities, served by volunteers.

Dan would tie the trees to the parking meter poles up and down the street outside the union hall. He wanted it to look a bit like Christmas as the Skid Row residents showed up for their Christmas dinner. He did this for a number of years.

For Dan, Christmas was not just another day, and the food inside the union hall was not another soup and bread line. And the men were not drunks or bums, homeless and alcoholics. This was not the day, the time, or the place to eat soup soaked in day old bread leaning up against a wall in an alley on a winter night.

Tying Christmas trees to parking meter poles

outside a union hall in the midst of Skid Row was a sign of something more about all human life. It was Christmas. It continues to be (for me) that 24-hour period of time that's says life can be something special for everyone ... from the bottom to the very top of the social ladder. We are all alike. No one is better. No one is worse.

It brings to my mind the words of our sacred text, *"God so loved that world that he sent His son to be among us..."*

So on one day, we want everyone fed, and no one left out. We want all the children gifted and loved. We want hate and discrimination, for just one day, to be eradicated by our generosity of time, treasure and talent. We want the poorest among us to be wrapped in a warm coat and dry socks, just like a Child who was wrapped in swaddling clothes. We want wars to cease and shootings to stop so that the proclamation of peace to all of good will can be made real.

We want a series of Christmas trees tied to parking meter poles to greet not just the down and out, but also to greet the dawn of a new day, a Christmas Day, when the light will out shine the darkness once and for all.

Dan, I never got the chance to thank you. I have no idea where you might be in the world today. But something tells me you are still a sign of hope to others this Christmas.

Merry Christmas, Dan.

Room in the Inn

"SISTER, IF THERE ARE A COUPLE OF KIDS who might not have a place to celebrate Christmas, my mom, dad, and I would be happy to have them in our home."

"Thanks, John, but right now it seems that we have place for everybody. But I will keep your offer in mind, if anything changes."

Change is a part of life. A few days later, I got a call.

"John, this is Sister Joette. If your offer still stands, we have a brother and sister who need a place to celebrate Christmas. Their parents informed us today that they are not able to take their kids this Christmas. I think you know Tommy from your work with the boys the last few years. His sister Kathy is a year younger."

"Sister, we would be happy to have them join our family for Christmas. Can I pick them up on Christmas Eve and return them on the 26th or 27th?"

"That would be wonderful, John. Just let us know about what time you might be arriving here. We will make sure they will be ready."

On Christmas Eve I crossed the city to picked up Tommy and his sister Kathy. They each had a small suitcase and off we went to celebrate Christmas together.

While we were driving to the Cusick house, my mom went shopping to buy a few gifts for each of the kids. After all, Christmas is about gifts!

On Christmas morning we went to Mass. When we returned home, we decided to open some gifts. Just as we were to begin, Tommy and Kathy went upstairs and came down with wrapped presents. They each had two gifts with Christmas labels. Each of the kids had purchased and wrapped gifts with "Mom" on one label and "Dad" on the other. They handed them to my mom and my dad, and said "Merry Christmas." They watched with smiles and joy as my mom and my dad unwrapped each one.

Try not to shed a few tears at the exchange.

My mom and dad made room in the Inn for two young people needing a place to stay. Tommy and Kathy fit in like they had lived with us for years. We had a wonderful few days together. My parents, especially my mom, loved kids. She delighted in their presence and enjoyed their company.

A problem arose when it was time to leave. They didn't want to go. A few days of experiencing some special love and personal attention were also gifts they received. They placed the gifts they received from us in their small suitcases and brought them downstairs to the living room and we put them in my car.

In the sacred Scripture the traditional translation is (for Mary and Joseph): *"There was no room in the Inn."* Another translation goes this way: *"There was no room in the place where travelers lodged."* I like to believe there was no room in that place for Joseph, Mary, and the Child because they were not travelers. They were home in Bethlehem, the House of Bread. Jesus is always home when He is with and among God's people.

Tommy and Kathy knew it was time to travel back to their living place. But for a little while mom, dad and I provided them a home where they could find love, welcome, kindness...and a few Christmas gifts!

As a matter of fact, we gifted each other in more ways than I ever imagined.

"She gave birth to her first-born son. She wrapped him in swaddling clothes and laid him in a manger because there was no room for them in the Inn."

When we make room for life and love, we will always experience the presence of God...sometimes in the birth of a Child; other times in people like Tommy and Kathy.

CHAPTER 10

Traditions

Chicago Traditions

FOR CHRISTMAS TO BE CHRISTMAS, there are many rituals I need.

I must walk by the Christmas windows in front of Marshall Field's. (Okay, it's now Macy's to you. It is still Marshal Field's to me.) I must travel to the 7th floor to see the Great Tree and to see if Uncle Mistletoe showed up this year.

I have added some new rituals. I need to walk over to the Daley Center and spend some time walking through the Christkindlmarket. And before I leave I must have a bratwurst (hold the kraut) and a glass of good German beer. And I year say a prayer for the people in Berlin who were walking through their Christkindelmarkt in 2016 and were killed or injured by a terrorist truck driver.

Then it is time to walk east on Randolph to Millennium Park and view Chicago's official Christmas tree. And, of course, I must stop and watch the ice skaters move around the rink below me. And last year I added a viewing of the ice ribbon and skaters that wind through Maggie Daley Park. I love to see the little kids just learning to skate and the young future speed skaters weave in and out of all the other skaters.

On Christmas Eve night, when all the stores begin to close, I will walk down Michigan Avenue to the river, cross the street and walk up the brightly-lit Magnificent Mile.

There is another ritual I wish I could still do: lunch at Berghoff's with my dad. I think my dad liked Berghoff's because this old German restaurant was awarded the first liquor license after Prohibition was repealed. And, of course, they brewed their own beer.

But there was an annual preamble to our lunch at Berghoff's. We would walk up State Street to Marshall Field's and take the elevator to the dress department. It was time to buy mom a Christmas gift.

To be blunt and to over-simplify, my father was a character. We would enter the dress department and make our way to a rack of nice dresses. A saleslady would greet us (astonishingly they really did in those days) and ask if she could help us.

My father, staring at the rack of nice dresses would point to one from about 20 feet away and tell her, "We will take that one." The saleslady looking rather surprised said, "Sir, do you want to look at that dress more closely?"

"No," my father replied, "But can you wrap it up nicely for us? You see, no matter which dress we choose, it will come back anyhow." And it always did! (Lesson for me since then: don't buy clothes for women.)

With the dress boxed with nice tissue paper and wrapped in Christmas paper in record time, it was placed in a green Marshall Field's bag. We walked back down State Street to Adams, turned right and entered Berghoff's. He had his beer and sausage. I had my coke and schnitzel. It was the Christmas season, and for this young guy, life was good.

Our annual Christmas ritual was completed! I had time with my dad. We bought a gift for mom. We hung out at Berghoff's. All was right and just in my part of the world.

I miss him. I miss that Pre-Christmas ritual.

But again this year. I will be at Berghoff's. In my dad's name it will be time for a beer and a sausage. Merry Christmas, dad. Merry Christmas, mom. Did you like the dress?

I pray for both of you again this Christmas. It is a Christmas ritual.

Having Our Christmas

"When are you going to have Christmas?"

"Now that's Christmas!"

"Daddy, is it Christmas yet?"

"Our Christmas is in helping others."

"We have Christmas on Sunday."

"We have two Christmases: here and at mom's."

"Now it's Christmas."

Christmas: it's an active word that describes so much: a season, an experience, an event, an attitude, a spirit. It's family, traditions, hopes, reality. Having our Christmas.

It is...the Great Tree, carols, Toys-for-Tots, poinsettias, *It's a Wonderful Life*, Hansel & Gretel, food drives, Santa Claus, *A Christmas Carol*, home for the holidays, the Salvation Army, The Magnificent Mile, *The Nutcracker*, *The Bells of St. Mary's*, Midnight Mass, "*God bless us everyone*," eggnog, the Neediest Children's

Fund, Rudolph the Red-Nosed Reindeer, *The Grinch Who Stole Christmas*. Sharing It. *Silent Night. O Holy Night.*

The symbols and experiences of Christmas pull out of us so much life: the closeness of love, the generosity of people, hopes for a better life, joy in the simple things, nothing taken for granted.

All of life is present at Christmas.

Every experience, every action, every moment seems to be found somewhere when we "Have our Christmas."

Remember its origin, those first experiences, the imagery and the words: angels and shepherds, swaddling clothes and manger, wise men and star, mother and child.

You have nothing to fear: *"A savior is born to you, the Messiah and Lord."*

All the experiences, then and now...all the symbols, then and now...reveal another experience: God is very close to us. Very, very close.

We are having our Christmas!

Midnight Mass

I ALWAYS ENJOYED Christmas Midnight Mass.

It began when I was an altar server. Our Pastor did not allow grade school kids to attend Midnight Mass. But when I was chosen to serve that Mass, I felt so grown up! The ritual of Midnight Mass and the Christmas music taking place from Midnight until 1:30 am captured me.

Now burned in my Christmas memory, Midnight Mass became an important part of my Catholic DNA. There is no other night in the year when Midnight Mass "works"—during the first hour of Christmas, 12/25.

As a kid I always pictured Jesus being born at night. Celebrating Catholic Mass at midnight, during the very first hour of Christmas, made sense to me. After all the Magi were following a star, and you can only see stars in the dark of a cloudless night.

In the early years of my priesthood, the four priests and deacon would gather around the altar at midnight with a packed church of people from our parish. It was wonderful. Kids were there with their families. We priests knew practically everyone at Midnight Mass. It was so special for all of us.

When my work moved me to our college seminary and concurrently to begin an outreach to young adults in their 20s and 30s, there was no longer a parish to pray with at Midnight Mass. The seminary students were all home in their own parishes. I felt lost.

So I began a new Midnight Mass tradition by reaching out to young adults, their families and friends. As the word got out, more and more people would be in attendance. I began to believe that by continuing to celebrate Midnight Mass I had found a new congregation: searchers and seekers. Many were seeking to recreate a Midnight Mass in which they participated earlier in life. Many did not have a parish at this time in life, but they had Faith.

I always tried very hard to make everyone feel welcome. I would never trash or admonish the "Christmas Catholic." When someone would say to me, "Father, it's been a long time since I've been to church," I'd just smile and say, "We don't take attendance." What a thrill it was for me to pray with them at Christmas Midnight Mass. They, too, have Faith.

By the mid-1980s Christmas Mass behavior was changing. Fewer parishes were celebrating Midnight

Mass. They began to substitute a Mass at 8:00 or 10:30pm. That made no sense to me. When asked "Why are you doing that?" the response usually was "The people are asking for that. They want a Christmas Mass earlier than midnight." I never bought that.

And I was discovering that I now had many more searchers and seekers at Midnight Mass.

When I moved downtown, I began celebrating Christmas Midnight Mass in one of the most beautiful and sacred chapels in Chicago: St James Chapel in the former Quigley Preparatory Seminary. It was never used at Christmas for over its 50-year history. It is located one block west of the trendy Magnificent Mile, Michigan Avenue. Four hundred plus people were present every Christmas Midnight.

I had no idea who many of them were. But it made no difference. They had Faith. And together we all prayed, and sang Christmas carols, and celebrated the Birth of Christ during the first hour of Christmas Day. We needed to do that. After all, it was a significant part of our Catholic DNA.

And for several years, before he retired, my Rabbi and his wife were in the first pew! They honored our Midnight Mass tradition and my faith with their presence.

When I retired in 2014, I also chose to retire from Midnight Mass. I am still torn inside with that decision. I simply could not stay up that late and function properly. I still get calls, emails, and texts inquiring about Midnight Mass. I just can't do it any longer. I miss it. I really do. Time marches on.

But I did not retire from my Faith or Christmas Mass. Not at Midnight, but on Christmas Eve or Christmas morning at Old St. Patrick's, I will stand at the altar of the Lord and proclaim that great piece of Sacred Scripture about a woman named Mary who gave birth to her first-born son, wrapped him in love and placed him in a manger, a feeding trough.

From the very beginning that Child was food for the people in God's world. From that manger I pretend I can hear the words "Come here. Take and eat. This is my Body given for you."

And I will continue on with Catholic Mass. I will come to the part of Mass where I will be privileged to stand in front of a long line of people, and one-by-one, eyeball-to-eyeball, I will look at each person and say four words to each one of them: "The Body of Christ." And once again that Child, once lying in that manger, will continue to be food for each and every person in that communion line at Christmas Mass.

And when I return to the altar, I will say quietly, "Thank you, Lord, thank you. Merry Christmas."

Speak It Out Loud!

ON CHRISTMAS EVE, 2016, I participated in something I had never done in my 46.5 years as a Catholic priest. I presided at Christmas Eve Mass at 5:00 pm.

I held out for many years, but this year for some reason (that is not well thought out) I have made myself available for Christmas Eve Mass.

When it comes to Christmas, I am a real traditionalist. Christmas is Christmas Day, December 25th each and every year. It is not December 24th, Christmas Eve, nor is it December 26th, in years the calendar says it is to be officially observed.

I have become more and more aware that Christmas has become a two-day event: Christmas Eve and Christmas Day. Special food, dinners, and a variety of activities begin one day and end the next. Many families experience two Christmas celebrations, one with each side of the family. And now that I think about that, so did our family. We celebrated with my dad's family on Christmas Eve and with mom's on Christmas afternoon.

Let's remember that whatever we do and with whomever we celebrate, there are two simple sentences that are the source for every Christmas celebration... from Mass in a gym or in a beautiful sacred space... to dinners, gifts, special cookies and cakes baked just once a year.

How about before all the hoopla begins, we stop for a moment and proclaim out loud these two sentences...

"While they were there the days of her confinement were completed. She gave birth to her first-born son and wrapped him in swaddling clothes and laid him in a manger, because there was no room in the inn."

1,000 Bad Christmas Trees

BUYING THE ANNUAL Christmas tree for our house was always a big deal. It always involved the three of us, mom, dad and me. It was never a simple procedure. It was a family outing that resembled a pilgrimage... journeying from Christmas tree lot to Christmas tree lot in search of the near-perfect tree.

One year, the tree pilgrimage almost ended my parents' marriage!

The three of us got in the family car, and my dad drove south on Western Avenue. We stopped at Crescent Landscaping. They had lots of Christmas trees. My dad was not a big Christmas tree "hunter." My mother was. She was in search of the "pearl of great price"—the perfect tree. Mom had German genes on both sides of her family!

We would process up and down aisles of fresh Christmas trees. She would stop at one and ask my dad or me to stand it up straight. She would examine the trunk and the shape. She would ask one of us to turn the tree around. She was looking to see if the tree had deformed or missing branches. Those were not permissible on a Christmas tree in the Cusick house.

After much searching at the Crescent Landscaping lot, my mother announced to my father and me, "They don't have any good ones."

I am about to smile and laugh again this year as I recall my dad's response.

Back on the sidewalk near the car my dad turned around, not looking at her, but facing all the Christmas trees. "Florence, the man must have 1,000 trees. You mean he has 1,000 bad trees?" Mom was furious!

Dad got back in the car, but now assumed the role of a taxi driver. Driving to the next tree lot, he said nothing and refused to get out of the car. Mom and I walked up and down the rows of trees, and I was the recipient of her anger and Christmas tree frustration with "your father!"

When she found the perfect tree, it was put in the trunk of the car, and the taxi driver drove us home. The family survived intact for one more year.

That experience popped into my head again this year as I unboxed the perfect (artificial) tree that now stands proudly in my living room. The tree is green, the trunk is still straight, the branches are as full as I could shape them...and all the lights work!

And for me, for another year, three of the religious

symbols of Christmas surround my tree:

The tree is "ever green"—the constant, unchanging color that reminds me of the constant unchanging Divine Presence that is a part of each one of our lives.

A silver star tops off the tree and my Christmas Crib is underneath. It was the star in the heavens that led the Magi to the Child with His mother.

And everything is in place once again. Come, Lord Jesus.

Rest in peace, mom and dad. It was a lot easier again this year to find the "perfect" Christmas tree. I went to the storage space and pulled it out of the box! And, dad, your line about the "1000 bad trees" came back to me, as it does every Christmas!

Merry Christmas to both of you!

CHAPTER 11

Sing with Me

The Hopes and Fears
of All the Years...

ONE MIDNIGHT MASS, over 30 years ago, left a permanent mark on my mind and memory.

I saw him come in the chapel and I made sure I went to his pew to welcome him personally. But it was when I was proclaiming the Gospel passage of the birth of Jesus and saw him standing head and shoulders taller than anyone around him that the reality hit me. He was a tall man. He stood above the crowd in many ways.

I was drawn to him after the Gospel and when I began my homily. He had a silly smile on his face. It was a smile of courage and conviction. It reminded me of someone who just crossed the finish line in a marathon: "I made it!"

Jim was a dying man. The cancer was killing him from the inside out. On that Christmas Eve, 1987, Jim made it to his most sacred night and event of the year.

Jim made it to Midnight Mass. His smile said it all. Surrounded by his family and in prayer with of us who know him, it was pretty clear that this would probably be his last Midnight Mass.

For many years, he believed in and lived out the mantra—One Day at a Time. He wasn't concerned about Midnight Mass, 1988. He made it to this sacred time. He made it to this Midnight Mass, 1987. That is what mattered the most. He lived in moment of our remembrance of the Birth of Christ.

One of the Christmas Carols that we all sang at Mass that night was "*O Little Town of Bethlehem.*" There are two lines in that Carol that shouted at me during that Mass: "T*he hopes and fears of all the years are met in Thee tonight.*"

In front of me, Jim sang those words because that night he was living those words. Weren't we all singing and living those words?

That is our Christmas faith. The good and the bad, our successes and failures, our life and our death...we connect spiritually to our Higher Power.

Beginning with the Child born in a manger, and journeying with that adult child, son of the Most High, to the outskirts of Jerusalem to wherever and live, work, and play today: "*The hopes and fears of all our years are met in Thee tonight.*"

How about we hum, sing, whistle or even sing a verse:

O little town of Bethlehem,
How still we see the lie!
Above thy deep and dreamless sleep
The silent stars go by;
Yet in thy dark streets shineth
The everlasting Light;
The hopes and fears of all the years
Are met in thee tonight.

Thanks, Jim. Sleep in heavenly peace.

...Are Met In Thee Tonight

AT A TIME LIKE THIS, in a place like this, with a people like this:

Christmas.

It makes you draw a much deeper breath, feel a little nervous, perhaps. Maybe profoundly grateful, sad, or hopeful.

It is a one of the most special times in all the year, a unique moment in human history.

Oh sure, it's an annual occurrence, but this day it doesn't feel like that. It's more solemn tonight than yearly, too special to count.

It's Christmas.

We will even sing it: *"The hopes and fears of all the years are met in Thee tonight."*

We look forward and backward—almost simultaneously. What will happen to us? Will we be blessed? Will it come out all right?

"You have nothing to fear. I come to proclaim good news to you. A Savior has been born to you."

167

What has happened to us? Why have we been so blessed? Why has it happened so?

"The hopes and fears of all the years are met in Thee tonight."

What has happened to us...is from the hand of God.

What will happen...is also in God's hands.

"The hopes and fears of all the years..."

The past, the present, what will come...

"...are met in Thee tonight."

At a time like this, in a place like this, with a people like this:

Something very special.

Christmas.

O Christmas Tree

No matter how difficult and changing life can become in the world, in our country, in our family, in our friends, and/or within us, do you believe that there is something among all these experiences that will never change?

The answer might be found in the meaning of the Christmas tree.

Many of the traditions that are a part of our celebration of Christmas have their origin in the northern areas of Christian Europe.

During this winter of the year, both in Northern Europe and here in the Midwest region of the U.S., the earth is pretty devoid of color with one big exception: evergreen trees. And the adjective says it all: ever-green. Those trees maintain the same color in the summer, fall, winter, and spring.

These non-color-changing, ever-green trees were cut down in the forests and found their way into people's homes as a part of the celebration of Christmas. Decorated with color and light, the never changing, ever present God so loved the world (us and everyone) that God sent his Son. Each tree in each home was a symbol that no matter what was happening in life, the divine presence that would never go away has made its way to be with, in, and among each one of us. The ever-green tree said it all.

The birth of the Child in Bethlehem speaks directly to that reality.

In many homes the symbol of the ever-green tree was enhanced by what people added to the top of the tree and placed underneath the tree. On the top you might place an angel or a star, and underneath the tree you might find a village or a crèche.

For years my manger scene had a prominent place under the tree. The spirit of our ever-loving God symbolized by star or angel comes down into the places where people live in the village and where the Christmas Child entered the world in Bethlehem. And what connects the two? The ever-green Christmas tree.

O Christmas Tree! O Christmas Tree!
Thy leaves are so unchanging;
Not only green when summer's here,
But also when 'it's cold and drear:
O Christmas Tree! O Christmas Tree!
Thy leaves are so unchanging.

O Christmas Tree! O Christmas Tree!
How richly God has decked thee.
O Christmas Tree! O Christmas Tree!
How richly God has decked thee.
O Christmas Tree! O Christmas Tree!

Your boughs can teach a lesson
That constant faith and hope sublime
Lend strength and comfort through all time
O Christmas Tree! O Christmas Tree!
Your boughs can teach a lesson.
"God so loved the world..."

Ever-green—the one thing that never changes! God's love.

It's Beginning to Look
a Lot Like Christmas....

GO AHEAD. Sing a verse with me...

It's beginning to look a lot like Christmas, Ev'rywhere you go;

Take a look in the five and ten glistening once again with candy canes and silver lanes aglow.

It's beginning to look a lot like Christmas, Toys in ev'ry store; but the prettiest sight to see is the holly that will be on your own front door.

(And buildings.) The "sounds of the season" surround us.

Bing Crosby, Charlie Brown, The Little Drummer Boy, and Jimmy Stewart make their annual appearances on screens of all sizes.

You can see a red-nosed reindeer, a red-suited man with gifts, bright-eyed children and an assortment of colored boxes adorned with ribbons and bows.

It's beginning to look a lot like Christmas...

Can you see the Child wrapped in love, lying in that manger as food for the entire world?

Can you see angels—not armies—announcing peace to you and all people of good will?

Can you see that Star in the night sky?

Can you see the light that "shines in the darkness, and the darkness has not overcome it?"

Can you see the birth of a Savior as vulnerable as a Child, yet a threat to the power of kings and emperors? Keep looking. The longer you look, the more you see.

It's beginning to look a lot like Christmas...

Sing a little more with me...

O Holy Night! The stars are brightly shining.
It is the night of the dear Savior's birth.
Long lay the world in sin and error pining.
Till He appeared and the soul felt its worth.
A thrill of hope the weary world rejoices
For yonder breaks a new and glorious morn.
Fall on your knees! Oh, hear the angel voices!
O night divine, the night when Christ was born
O night divine, O Night, O night divine!
And when we sing O Come, O Come Emmanuel...
Let us all Rejoice! Rejoice!

May God be with us for a truly Merry Christmas!